C000095503

FINDING REFUGE

Finding Refuge

*Love in a time of
Lockdown*

TONY HORSFALL

Charis Training

CONTENTS

| 1 |

Foreword

In 2019 Tony and I co-wrote a book on resilience. Writing is one thing. Living it out is quite different.

2020 has brought challenges for most of us. For Tony it has been a time of twists and turns; hospice, care home and hospital; fighting for his life when he developed COVID-19, and the death of his beloved wife Evelyn. His resilience has certainly been put to the test.

This book contains Tony's reflections as he wrote them in a blog at the time. As his friends read them, we cried, and we sometimes laughed (especially reading about his virtual church experiences). Amidst suffering and sorrow, Tony brings hope and love. The love he has for Evelyn; love from nurses, doctors, carers and chaplains; love shown by friends; and overall, the love of God. In the darkest of times, Tony draws deeply from the Bible and brings out new insights. He demonstrates how the Scriptures remain relevant to daily life today.

Tony is a man of integrity and writes with honesty. We can all learn from the way in which he faces challenges and keeps going, trusting in God. Let's learn to love more deeply.

I recommend this book to you if you want to be uplifted and encouraged, as we journey through difficult times.

Dr Debbie Hawker, clinical psychologist

acknowledgement

Thanks to Kat Gibson for permission to use her painting 'Togetherness' as the cover for this book.

| 2 |

PROLOGUE

Like everyone else in the world we did not expect 2020 to bring a global pandemic. Nor did we anticipate the havoc it would cause in our lives.

My wife Evelyn and I assumed the new year would mean the continuation of weekly visits to the hospital for her chemotherapy, something we had been doing since 2016 when she had a recurrence of breast cancer. The diagnosis then was that the cancer was 'not curable but containable'. Bravely she had endured round after round of treatment with various drugs, each with its own side-effects. Three time she lost her hair; her fingernails and toenails turned black, and she developed painful lymphoedema in her left arm. She faced this suffering with calmness and courage, never complaining, never feeling sorry for herself.

Then in February came the news we had feared. The cancer had spread to her spine. The consultant told us there was no more treatment available, and that she now had only months to live. Evelyn had a quick, concentrated course of radiotherapy to try and slow down the spread of the disease and we began to adjust our thinking as to what might lie ahead.

At the same time my 70th birthday was on the horizon in March. We decided to go ahead with a small celebration for our closest friends and family, to be followed the next day by an after-church buffet so we could share with our friends there. That was something special to look forward to, and our son Alistair and his family decided to come over from Australia to be with us. Little did we know on that March weekend just how suddenly our lives would be changed, and how drastically. Lockdown began immediately afterwards, and it was the last time we met together as a church for many months. Alistair had to rush back to Australia to avoid being stranded in the UK. And Evelyn's condition began to rapidly decline.

What follows is the account of the next four months told through my postings on Facebook. I have always found journaling a good way to process thoughts and feelings. Writing has been for me a source of release and a way of trying to make sense of what is happening in my life. It also became a valuable point of contact with people around the world who wanted to pray for us as they saw our story unfold. So, whenever I could I posted on my Facebook page any thoughts I had that I considered might be worth sharing.

Now I want to share those thoughts with you, just as they were written at the time. I have deliberately not polished them up in any way, simply adding a few more words for clarification. For the main they are exactly as they appeared on Facebook.

My hope is that, as you share our journey, you will find inspiration to face your own challenges, whatever they are. For sure, none of us are without personal trials and all of us face adversity in one form or another. But we can learn from each other's experience, and of course, scripture is there to guide us through our times of testing. So my prayer is that through the combination of personal testimony and Biblical reflection that you will find here your faith will be strengthened and you will find your way through the difficulties. Above all, my prayer is that God will be glorified.

| 3 |

FROM HOME TO THE HOSPICE

22nd March
PLANS, PLANS, PLANS (1)
"For I know the plans I have for you," declares the Lord, "plans to prosper you and not to harm you, plans to give you a hope and a future (Jeremiah 29:11)."

This is a season when 'all the best-laid plans of mice and men' are coming to naught. Like me, you will have experienced disappointment that things you were looking forward to will not now take place. Life has fallen into a vacuum with nothing to hold it together. It feels strange and unnerving not to be in control.

However, this scripture reminds us that God's plans remain firm and secure. We may not know what is happening next, but God does, and his plans for us (and his church, and his world) remain safe and reliable. Try to rest today in this glad assurance that a bigger purpose is at work in your circumstances. You are not at the mercy of chance or fate, or some hitherto unknown virus. The Almighty God holds you safe in the palm of his hand, and even now his perfect will is being worked out. You may not understand, but he certainly does. "I know the plans I have for you," declares the Lord.

23rd March

PLANS, PLANS, PLANS (2)

"For I know the plans I have for you," declares the Lord, "plans to prosper you and not to harm you, plans to give you a hope and a future (Jeremiah 29:11)."

In times of turmoil and unprecedented uncertainty it is good to hold on to the fact that God's plans are unchanging and unstoppable. The plans he has for us are good plans, to prosper us and not to harm us.

For many this is a season of economic hardship as jobs are lost and income decreased. We need to hear this reminder that God is our Provider, whose name is Jehovah-Jireh (Genesis 22:14). Here is an opportunity to see how God will meet and supply all our needs (Philippians 4:19). As with Elijah at the brook Cherith, he will command his ravens to feed us (1Kings 17:4). To prosper in this context is simply to have all that we need – no more, no less. The Lord will provide.

It is also a time of fear, even of panic, and the threat of getting sick or even dying stalks the land. God's good plan is to protect us so that we are not harmed by anything that may befall us. This does not mean some heavenly immunity to sickness or trouble, but the promise that we will come through it, and that whatever happens will only serve to bring about the good purpose of God in our lives (Romans 8:28). There is much for us to learn in these days, about God and his ways and about ourselves and our need for transformation.

Humble dependency on God and a heartfelt gratitude for small mercies towards the One who is both Provider and Protector will be a great outcome from this time of trial for those whose trust is in him.

24th March

PLANS, PLANS, PLANS (3)

"For I know the plans I have for you," declares the Lord, "plans to prosper you and not to harm you, plans to give you a hope and a future (Jeremiah 29:11)."

God has plans for our lives, and his plans are for our good. These eternal purposes are full of gracious plans, bringing into our lives more than we could ever have expected or imagined. As with the people of Israel, who had been disciplined by God and taken into exile as a result of their persistent sinfulness, we too may well have fallen short of God's standards in one way or another. But always his response to us is one of grace, giving us what we could never deserve or merit.

Perhaps you are on the point of despair, and feeling that all hope is gone? In times of isolation and loneliness it is easy to fall into depression and, like Pilgrim, to find ourselves in the Slough of Despond. All seems lost, everything seems dark. That is when we need to remember that God's gracious plan can give us hope. His good purpose for us will not be defeated. However far we have fallen he will lift us up again, for he is the God of all grace.

Furthermore, we can look to the future with confidence. The present may be difficult, and the future full of uncertainty from a human perspective, but he is the One who holds the future and he will bring us through. Just as he brought Israel home again from exile in Babylon, so he will restore us after this time of isolation and loss. One day we will look back on this period of history and marvel at all that the Lord has done in us, and for us, and through us.

The Lord Almighty has sworn, "Surely, as I have planned, so it will be, and as I have purposed, so it will stand." (Isaiah 14:24)

1st April

Many of you know that I have been caring for my wife Evelyn at various levels over the past four years as she has battled with breast cancer. In February the cancer spread to her spine, and this meant I became her full-time carer, which has been an honour and privilege. However, her needs have increased, and I am no longer able to give her the care she needs, so we have taken the decision for her to go into a Care Home. This was a heart-rending decision since the implication was that we would not be able to see her again because of visiting restrictions due to the virus. Then my brother-in-law suggested we might go in together. Amazingly, two rooms were found for us at Cherry Trees, a Care Home near Barnsley, and we expect to go there later today.

These have been difficult and lonely days for us as, like everyone else, we have felt the pain of isolation at a time when we most needed the emotional and practical support of friends and family. But God has not failed us or left us unnoticed.

As Evelyn comes to the end of her earthly pilgrimage, the scripture that has come to strengthen us is this: "For to me, to live is Christ and to die is gain (Philippians 1:21)." This sums up her life, lived since childhood for the glory of God, and is the foundation for our hope that when this life ends, heaven awaits – something which is far better than life on planet earth.

I am not sharing this for dramatic effect, to elicit sympathy, or to seek attention. Just to let you know this is our situation right now. Difficult days are still ahead, so what we most value is your prayer – that we may have peace and be able to rest in Jesus.

2nd April

A STING IN THE TAIL

When Evelyn arrived at the Care Home by ambulance yesterday afternoon she was turned away because her temperature was too high. This is more likely due to her overall condition, but they did not want to risk her having the virus, so she was brought home again. Imagine our disappointment when everything had seemed to be working so well. Our daughter Debbie and I are back to caring for her at home, but there is a glimmer of hope for which we ask your prayers - the local hospice may be willing to take her today or tomorrow. Her temperature has come down now, so that will help. I am reluctant to get my hopes up though after yesterday's disappointment. I think I may be able to join her there if it works out, but not yet certain. Being in the hospice would be our preferred option. We are overwhelmed by the messages of support.

2nd April (2nd posting)

A SILVER LINING.

It's amazing! Here we are in the hospice, and I can stay too! We got a call from them just before 9am and by 10am the ambulance had been and collected her, and 30 minutes later we were here. What an amazing provision. I woke at 6am this morning full of apprehension at what the day would bring; now I can feel the tension of the last few weeks slowly draining from my body! Ev is sleeping peacefully and soon the doctor will come to see her. We are no longer alone. Debbie, our daughter, has gone home to her family and her work having said what may be a final goodbye to her mum since no visitors are allowed at the hospice due to the virus. We are so grateful to God for each of you. I hope you are encouraged by this good outcome.

3rd April

A good first night in the hospice, we both slept well. Evelyn in one of those super hospital beds, I am on an armchair recliner next to her. I imagined I was flying to Singapore and had been upgraded from economy to Business Class. That helped! The doctor yesterday was superb. He had her medical history at his fingertips, and we felt so safe. We have met 4 nurses with whom Evelyn worked in the past and who knew her as 'Sister' in the nursing home where she was senior staff some years ago. The doctor asked routinely, "Do you have any kind of faith?" Evelyn replied, "Well I know I'm going to heaven!" He seemed satisfied.

4th April

I wrote these words many months ago for a book of daily readings, and I find myself reading them again today.

Presence

"Even though I walk through the valley of the shadow of death, I will fear no evil, for you are with me(Psalm 23:4)."

All this took place to fulfil what the Lord said through the prophet: "The virgin will be with child and will give birth to a son, and they will call him Immanuel" – which means, "God is with us (Matthew 1:22-23)."

A friend was diagnosed with an aggressive form of breast cancer, which required radical surgery. Leading up to the operation she had been fine, buoyed by the prayers of her friends and family, but as she waited for surgery she had a panic attack. All she could think of was to breathe deeply and slowly, and to repeat aloud to herself, 'God is with us, God is with us.'

At that moment she heard voices in the next cubicle. The doctor was introducing himself to the patient. 'Hello,' he said, 'my name is Dr Emmanuel, and my name means 'God is with us." It was an amazing moment of confirmation that God was truly with her in her time of need. This incident instilled in her a sense of God's presence that calmed her fears and carried her through the long weeks of treatment still ahead of her.

The Psalmist also reminds us that in the darkest valley, God is with us, and we need not be afraid. Whatever you are facing today, say with confidence, 'God is with me, God is with me.' (1)

4th April (second posting)

When I can I am reading the book of Ruth, with its emphasis on the providence of God, which refers to the outworking of his good purpose in the world, and in our lives. I came across this in the course of my reading just now:

"Such belief in God's providence gives a firm standpoint from which to seek to understand the world. We do not see the glories and the tragedies of national and global events, and the joys and pains of family life, as finding their meaning only within human history or personal biography. Their true meaning lies within the purposes of a God who has made himself known as loving and holy, as personal and infinite, as Creator and Redeemer, as Sustainer and Ruler. Human joys are thus enriched . . . But the uncertainties of life, too, are brought within the context of a faith by which they may be coped with. . . 'Providence' says that God is there, God cares, God rules, and God provides." (2)

I'm trying to live by this truth, and to rest in it, day-by-day at the moment.

5th April

A headline in the local newspaper highlights the cash crisis being faced by the hospice since many of their funding sources have dried up during lockdown. Their charity shops have had to close, and all fundraising events are cancelled.

Would you consider making a small donation at this crucial time? All treatment is free, they depend on giving from those who see the value of palliative care.

6th April

Evelyn has had a good night and her condition continues to improve with the great care she is receiving here. A little TLC goes a long way. We have been very impressed with the staff all of whom remain cheery despite the challenge of staff shortages. One nurse yesterday almost passed out in our room from the effect of working with a mask on; others are working 14 hour shifts to cover for absent colleagues; all are doing additional and unfamiliar duties, but not complaining. Ev is now impatiently waiting for breakfast, her appetite increased by the steroids she is on. It's a good sign.

8th April

Decisions will be taken today as to whether or not we can continue to have a place here in the hospice now that Evelyn's condition has stabilised. It could mean that we will move to Cherry Trees Care Home after all. It is a vulnerable time for us both, which is why today's reading is special. Again, my own words written many months ago, come back to speak to me.

Goodness

"Surely goodness and love will follow me all the days of my life (Psalm 23:6)."

"Praise the Lord, O my soul; all my inmost being, praise his holy name. Praise the Lord, O my soul, and forget not all his benefits (Psalm 103:1-2)."

I have often said that if ever I write an autobiography, I will call it '*All the days of my life*', using the words from this verse.

Looking back over our lives and reflecting on the key moments is actually a very helpful thing to do, not simply because of nostalgia, but for reminding oneself of the goodness of God. Many things are best seen with hindsight. Often events we thought had gone wrong turn out to have been for the best. With a backward glance we can see how the providence of God has shaped circumstances for our good, even though they may have been painful at the time. All of this helps us to appreciate the goodness of God in its many and varied expressions. As you ponder this, what examples from your own story come to mind?

This reminder of past goodness is a great encouragement when we face an uncertain future. The God who is faithful, and has been faithful, will continue to be faithful, no matter what. As the hymn writer Joseph Hart (1712-1764) says, 'We'll praise him for all that is past, And trust him for all that's to come.' (3)

8th April (second posting)

We are so grateful for the many prayers offered on our behalf, and for your good wishes at this time. We will move tomorrow from the hospice to a Care Home, Cherry Trees in Monk Bretton (near Barnsley) where we originally were going. We will have a room each there and are at peace about this decision. Evelyn will be receiving nursing care, I will be a temporary resident. We have not visited the home before, so are going, like Abraham, not knowing where we are heading, but we do believe that God is guiding us. We have received outstanding care here, and it is difficult to leave a place where we have felt so safe and secure, so tomorrow will not be easy. But the promise is, "as your days so shall your strength be (Deuteronomy 33:25, NKJV)."

| 4 |

CHERRY TREES (Part 1)

10th April

You may notice that this is being written rather early in the morning. The transition from the calm efficiency of the hospice with its newly renovated rooms and highly professional staff to the noise and busyness of a typical Barnsley Care Home is indeed a stark one. We are suffering culture shock. It reminds me of my first visits to Africa when everything seemed strange and disorientating and my heart cried, 'I want to go home.' But we will learn to adapt, to adjust our expectations, find the rhythm of this place, look for the good, and learn to be content.

The main thing is that we are together.

We have been helped by some special tokens of God's love. A parcel waiting for us on our arrival, several items to make our stay that bit brighter, each individually wrapped and chosen with great care, plus a card with a beautifully prophetic message; a food parcel dropped off by friends with goodies from M&S; a hand written note from friends with the most beautiful writing, itself a message of love. These all helped to soften the blow.

My main concern is that Ev will get the care she needs. I have my own room, further down the corridor, so I will get dressed in a moment and go and see how her first night has been. She is adjusting better than I am because she has worked in the Care sector all her life, but she is still very vulnerable and dependent on those around her.

The Social Care sector has always been neglected in Britain, and right now the focus is almost solely on the wonderful NHS. But there is an army of other, very ordinary people, doing their best to care for the most vulnerable and helpless of people. We should celebrate our Care workers too, who are working against great odds to look after those with the most challenging of needs.

11th April

One of the principles of good cross-cultural adjustment that I have taught many times over the years is that of learning to trust your hosts in the new culture. This is not always easy of course since our level of mistrust or suspicion can be very high. It seems to me that settling into life in the Care Home requires us to trust our hosts. To trust that they know their job and will do it well. That means giving the right medication at the right time, responding to any call for help, keeping an eye on things and so on. So far, so good, so our trust level is rising. Evelyn was finding the air mattress she was on very uncomfortable and noisy. When we asked if it could be changed the nurse arranged this straight away. Evelyn slept well last night as a result and is more at peace. Trust is growing. And yesterday the home in general seemed calmer and quieter, for which we are thankful.

12th April

DRINKING THE MILK OF HUMAN KINDNESS

Perhaps you know this expression. It refers to the human ability to be kind and compassionate towards others who are less fortunate. It first appears in Shakespeare's *Macbeth*, where Lady Macbeth laments her husband's lack of ruthlessness, saying he is 'too full of the milk of human kindness.'

One of the positive things to emerge during the pandemic is a new wave of human kindness. It is a global phenomenon, people choosing to act compassionately towards neighbours and friends, not because they must, but because they choose to. When people act in this way, and display kindness, they are in fact displaying a quality of God, who himself is always kind. It shows that there is something of the image of God in every person if they choose to release it.

In the story of Ruth in the Bible - which I am trying to study when I have the chance and the motivation - Boaz shows such kindness to the destitute widow Ruth by allowing her to glean in his field, protecting her from abuse, and providing water for her to drink.

One of the things that Evelyn has noticed about the staff here in the Care Home is that they are for the most part very kind people, and it means a lot to us since we are dependent upon their good will. When you are caring for high dependency people day in, day out, it is easy to become jaded, to cease to care as a means of self-protection and simply go through the motions. The sparkle of kindness can be missing. Fortunately, we have been on the receiving end of much kindness here at Cherry Trees, and hopefully our gratitude shows through.

Perhaps today you too can offer another person the milk of human kindness?

13th April

AT LEAST WE ARE TOGETHER

This has been our mantra over the last few troublesome weeks. In all the ups and downs, in all the changes, in the emotional highs and lows, we have been strengthened by our faith and the fact that we are together. Our life verse, from Ecclesiastes 4:9-12 says that two are better than one, and this is still our experience.

A friend sent us a card for our arrival here at Cherry Trees, from one of her paintings called 'Togetherness.' That was wonderful enough, but inside was a beautiful Blessing she had penned for us. I wanted to share it with you here.

May you know the comfort, friendship and closeness of Jesus even more beautifully than before.

May He delight your heart and refresh your spirit each day, and may His presence nourish you.

May He hold you and speak with you in all the change, grief and yearning, and may His love be like a waterfall surrounding you.

Beautiful isn't it? May it be Lord, may it be!

14th April

BOUNDARIES

I have compared moving into Cherry Trees to entering a new culture. Such a transition involves learning new social norms and accepting certain boundaries or limitations.

Cherry Trees is a big place, built on three levels. Evelyn's room overlooks a pleasant garden and during the hot weather of the Easter weekend (10th - 12th) I thought I would enjoy some fresh air for a while. I managed to find my way down and sat contentedly beneath the shady trees. On my return however I was invited into the 'office' and told in no uncertain terms that during the lockdown the garden was out of bounds to me and that I should stay on the middle floor. Isolation within isolation! It was a blow to my freedom, but understandable since the danger of the spread of the virus in a Care Home is extremely high and the consequences unthinkable. Sometimes for the greater good we must limit ourselves. Compared to the Hospice, where we were literally confined to one room, here I have plenty of freedom. There is an area of decking that overlooks the car park where I can enjoy fresh air, and I can walk the long corridors freely. It was a learning experience. These are unusual times and most of us must accept limitations to our freedom and practice self-discipline. Only then can the pandemic be defeated, and freedom be restored.

15th April

FEELINGS

Just a week ago, when we were still at the Hospice, the doctor asked Evelyn a routine question: "How are you feeling today?" She replied quickly, with a one-word answer: "Down".

I was shocked, because in 46 years of marriage I have never heard her say anything like that. She is normally so placid, so even-tempered. In the many ups and downs of our life Evelyn has always been the steady one, the rock. I am the one given to emotional fluctuations. This was unusual, out of character even, and it worried me.

On asking her afterwards what was troubling her it seemed to be the loss of control of even the most basic aspects of life, the inability to shape the outcome of things. "If anyone said to me, 'What have you done today?' I would have to say, "Well, I waited for breakfast, then I waited for tablets, then I waited for a bed bath."

Yesterday she was unusually quiet, and I sensed she was sad, feeling again this chronic loss of control. We spend a lot of time waiting, dependent on others to do what you need them to do for you, people who are exceptionally busy and responding to the urgent needs of so many others.

Waiting is often presented as a deeply spiritual approach to life, but in reality, it is often at the root of our sense of loss, of our grief. No wonder feelings of sadness are never far away. Nor are such feelings easy to throw off. It needs an act of grace, an infusion of divine joy, and faith and trust.

Lord grant that to us for this day's waiting, Amen.

16th April

A VERY BUSY DAY

Yesterday turned out to be a very full day. Yes, there was plenty of 'waiting' to be done, but two significant things happened.

First a visit from a Community Nurse reminding us that if we wanted Evelyn could receive care at home, with carers coming in 4 times a day to look after her. It is a tempting possibility to have the comforts of home and the joy of our own garden again. We pondered this all morning but, in the end, decided against it for several reasons. In the present climate there is no guarantee that such a level of care can be provided consistently, and it would still leave me alone and responsible, especially at night. On the other hand, we have done the hard work of settling in here at Cherry Trees. We are well cared for and have no need to worry about meals or laundry, we have company and 24-hour care. So, we decided to stay here, despite the threat that Care Homes are under from the virus. It is a risk we have to take.

Then in the afternoon, with the help of a hoist and sling, Evelyn was able to sit in a chair for an hour, her first time out of bed for two weeks. She loved being able to see things from this new perspective and being able to read the paper easily again. It lifted her mood as well, and hopefully this will now be part of her daily routine.

We felt your prayers for us were being answered yesterday. Now it is important to pray that this and other Care Homes, are protected from the virus. The staff have done such a good job of sealing the place off. May it continue to be virus-free.

17th April
DISTORTIONS

In these abnormal times I guess we are all aware of how different life feels and how hard it is to keep our bearings. The normal markers are missing.

- Here at Cherry Trees we are less than 5 miles from home, but home feels a million miles away, as if it were in another universe.
- Today is Friday (I think) but every day feels the same, and one day merges into another.
- We have been here a week, but it feels like a month.
- It's about 7.30am, but time seems to pass very slowly and the days are long.

It is easy to feel that God has forgotten us, that we are on our own, but that too is a massive distortion. He will never leave us nor forsake us. We may not feel his Presence, but it is there, and that is the key truth to hold on to when everything else feels strange and unusual.

18th April
WHAT FRIENDS ARE FOR

We have only known Steve and Christina since November, but they have become good friends. When they offered to do anything to help us, I doubt if they imagined this assignment - collecting a commode from our home, washing it with bleach and then delivering it to Cherry Trees. We really appreciate their help.

19th April

THE LORD'S DAY

Today is Sunday, the Lord's Day, when we remember that Christ not only died, but rose again. Sin has been dealt with and death defeated.

According to my diary I should have been heading to Spain this afternoon to lead a retreat at El Palmeral, a wonderful villa just outside Alicante. A worldwide pandemic and our personal circumstances meant that we have known for some time that this would not happen. It is a disappointment that many others have felt when events we have looked forward to have been cancelled. So instead of leading a group of friends old and new in thinking about being more *Attentive to God*, I find myself at Cherry Trees and seeking to discern his presence in an unlikely setting.

Yesterday was a difficult day when Evelyn sank a little deeper into the harsh realities of her condition. She is no longer able to manage her basic bodily functions and this became a messy and emotionally painful reality as the day wore on. Coming to terms with this loss of dignity is embarrassing and humbling all round, but how we thank God for the skill and compassion of her carers - Louise and Nichola during the day and Leanne and David overnight. They were so good with her, unperturbed by what was happening and helping her come to terms with it.

As Christians we have no monopoly on kindness and compassion. These good people have been Christ to us in our time of need. Their shifts are long and demanding, they are pulled this way and that, but they remain calm and considerate. Often, they are abused by the more disturbed residents, both physically and verbally. They have my utmost respect and our sincere thanks.

Pray that we will be able to manage this new reality with grace and peace. God knows our need.

20th April

WHERE IS GOD WHEN YOU NEED HIM MOST?

Don't worry, I have not lost my faith. Nor is this a rant about the injustice of God. I don't feel God has deserted me, abandoned me, mistreated me or neglected me. On the contrary, I am surrounded my many tangible evidences of his love - texts, messages, emails, phone calls, cards, gifts, and flowers all bring the same message: God is with us in this difficult period. No, my problem is not with God but with myself, and my own inability to connect with him as I did before.

We received the diagnosis that Evelyn's cancer had spread into her spine in mid-February, when we were also told that her prognosis was 'months not years'. Since then life has been different and my ability to focus and concentrate on God has nose-dived, just when I need to take hold of him the most.

The first indication of this came when I realised I would not manage to preach at church when I was next on the rota. I simply could not bring my thoughts together even though I had a rough idea of what I wanted to say. Fortunately, someone else stood in for me. Since then I have found it difficult to pray. Even though so many are praying for me, I seem to lack the focus and concentration to follow my normal prayer routine. Life has lost its shape, its rhythm.

Likewise, my study of Scripture has slipped. I felt I might study the book of Ruth, and I have begun to ponder this beautiful story, but mostly through the books I have brought with me than through my own insights or reading. And again, it has been spasmodic, and a bit hit and miss.

So, at the moment I am being carried on the faith and prayers of others, and I guess this is alright for now. I have occasional glimpses of how it used to be which encourage me to think this is a temporary blip. I know that it is God's hold on me that counts, not my hold on him. But it is an interesting insight into the nature of the spiritual life. Sometimes all we can do is rest and be carried along.

21st April

STRUCTURE AND RHYTHM

A mental health specialist says that structure is essential to well-being. Certainly I think some of my own difficulties have been because the normal structure of my life has fallen apart over the last month. Everything has been about seeing to the urgent and the shape has been lost. I guess this period of lockdown will have affected others in a similar way.

When I think of the major changes that have happened to us recently I should not be surprised. We were living in our own home, then the hospice, now Cherry Trees. And with each move we are adjusting to new people and a new routine, lacking privacy and no longer able to shape our days.

However, we have now been at Cherry Trees for 12 days and we are beginning to discern the pattern of each day. Everything revolves around mealtimes (9 breakfast, 12.30 lunch, 4.30 tea, 8.30 supper) so we are not lacking for food! In between there is an order for giving out medications and personal care of patients. Surprisingly the days are full. Movement starts early about 6am and doesn't finish until about 10.30 at night.

In between this we can find pools of stillness if we try hard. I like this time, 7 to 8 am and I have found writing these notes really helpful in processing my thoughts. At other times during the day

I may read some Bible notes or my commentary on Ruth - as well as doing word puzzles, colouring, and a bit of exercise on the decking attached to this unit. Evelyn is usually washed and dressed after breakfast and then with the help of a hoist transferred to a recliner chair next to her bed. She enjoys the upright position and being able to see the comings and goings. We watch a bit of TV and talk to the staff when they have time.

I am so grateful for the assurances of prayer that were given by friends yesterday and for the reminders that this is a period when it is ok for us to be carried on the prayers of others. I feel more relaxed about it all now and will seek to live one day at a time. I hope you are managing to find structure and rhythm in these chaotic days. It certainly helps our sense of well-being.

22nd April

NOISE

In the outside world it is being said that the lockdown and lack of traffic movement is leading to a quieter world where people can hear the birds sing again. I'm so pleased to hear that, and I hope you are taking advantage of the new conditions.

Anyone who has experience of Care Homes will know they are by contrast noisy places. Day or night something is happening. Phones ring unanswered and buzzers buzz without response. People talk loudly as if everyone is deaf. Radios are on full volume with pop songs blaring out from open doors. TV programmes vie for attention, their presenters calling out into a vacuum of disinterest. A man cries out. A lady sings. The breakfast trolley squeaks past as folks begin to gather in the dining room. Someone swears, unhappy to be herded along at such an early hour. Good morning Britain.

Amazingly after a while we adjust to the noise level and begin to tune it out. Like people living next to a busy main road we no longer hear the noise in the same way. And we can always close the door. Thank God for a heavy fire door that shuts us off for a while and encloses us in something like quietness.

Didn't Jesus say that when we pray we should 'Shut the door?' I love silence. I need silence. Like my body needs vitamins my soul needs silence. So, I am grateful for every quiet moment we can have together even if all we do is to sit in companionable silence.

Make the most of whatever silence comes your way today. The world will not always be this quiet.

23rd April

DEEP CALLS TO DEEP

The psalmist recognised that in the turbulence of his own experience God was inviting him into a deeper relationship of faith and trust. "In the roar of your waterfalls, all your waves and breakers have gone over me," he says starkly (Psalm 42:7). It seems that God uses the troublesome times in our lives to take us deeper into his heart, if we choose to go there.

That is certainly how it feels to me right now. In my present circumstances I have an opportunity to find God more deeply. These days of restriction and limitation in Cherry Trees, of sitting alongside Evelyn in her need, can change me for the better and shape me for the future if I so wish. And I do (I think).

Hopefully when all this is over - and it will come to an end - I will emerge as a different person. My hair will be longer, my eyebrows thicker and my waist enlarged, but hopefully my soul will have been refined and purified too. I want to be more compassionate, more dependent, more humble, more grateful, and more aware of others.

Meanwhile the Home seems to be under siege right now and fighting a battle for survival. The defences against the virus have been stepped up, which means more work even when there is less staff. For the 12-hour shift yesterday we had 2 carers instead of 3.

They worked incredibly hard the whole day on this nursing unit. I am so glad that many are praying for us here, and for similar situations through the country. It is perhaps the new frontline in the fight against the corona virus.

24th April
STAND BY ME
You must be wondering how I spend my time here. Are the days long? Do I get bored? Would I rather be at home?

Well my job here is to be Evelyn's companion, friend and lover. I am not her carer and must leave that to others. My task is to be with her and help her as much as I can.

I spend the night in my own room but aim to be with Ev by about 7am when she is usually just surfacing from sleep. Depending on how she is, she may sleep a bit more or I may make a drink for us - coffee for Ev, tea for me. I may arrange her pillows to make her more comfortable, even give her a little face wash. Then we are fairly quiet until breakfast comes about 9am when I make sure she can manage to eat and drink.

During the morning I pass on messages from different friends. We may call Alistair in Perth or watch a bit of TV. At some point she will be moved from bed into her day chair and maybe have her clothes changed. I may go out to the decking to get some fresh air and a little exercise.

After lunch we both have a rest. I find myself negotiating with the carers as to Evelyn's needs, more reminders than anything else. There may be little jobs to do, like today, trimming some flowers we received. Of course, we talk, sometimes in depth, sometimes just generally. Ev may doze and I may too, unless I am reading or doing a crossword. I try to keep up with emails, Facebook messages and WhatsApp, a job in itself. We will have a call from Evelyn's brother

Ian, and probably from Debbie to keep in touch. So the day goes by. Sometimes it is an easy day, sometimes there are challenges.

The night staff come on about 8pm and will give Ev her tablets, then get her ready for bed. I go back to my room after 9pm and may watch something on my iPad or read my Kindle. By 10pm I am ready for bed and usually sleep well.

We are both deeply conscious of how we are being upheld by prayer. That we have settled so well is amazing really, also that Evelyn is not in any pain. But we live one day at a time and try not to take anything for granted. "As your days, so shall your strength be" remains our watchword (Deuteronomy 33:25).

25th April

MY TEARS HAVE BEEN MY FOOD

I've cried a lot over the past few weeks. At one point anything could set me off - a memory, a disappointment, a fear about the future, an act of kindness . . . For a while it felt like there was a huge sponge full of emotion inside me, and if it was touched in any way water in the form of tears would flow out.

This could happen at any time and was beyond my control - during a phone call, when speaking to the doctor, whenever I prayed with Ev.

Thankfully I am not so 'teary' now, which shows how healing it has been for us here at Cherry Trees, and how sustained we have been by your prayers and words of encouragement. But I am not ashamed of my tears. Tears are healing. Tears are releasing. Tears are a natural expression of love, compassion and caring, a healthy response to grief, loss and sadness. They are not a sign of weakness or of an inability to cope, but of our humanity and being real.

Jesus wept (John 11:35). He cried when his friend Lazarus died, he wept over Jerusalem, he wept in the Garden. He understands tears, he is not embarrassed by our crying. He knows, he cares, he understands. He is "a man of suffering, and familiar with pain (Isaiah 53:3)."

These are difficult days for many. Don't be surprised if some days you are emotionally fragile. Let the tears flow and don't suppress them. Everyone feels better for a good cry.

26th April

MISSING YOU

One of the reasons that the Psalmist became depressed was because he could no longer meet with others in worship. In Psalm 42, he looks back wistfully to those days when he would lead the great temple processions. Now he is alone and isolated, probably in Exile (v4): 'These things I remember as I pour out my soul: how I used to go to the house of God under the protection of the Mighty One with shouts of joy and praise among the festive throng.' He feels flat and emotionally low.

Today we would normally be at church, and although we will have an online service which we will enjoy, it will not be the same as actually being together. In these days of lockdown and isolation I really miss my church friends - our brothers and sisters in Christ. I miss seeing them, hearing their voices, talking with them, giving them a hug.

Worship is essentially an interactive, corporate affair. A spiritual dynamic is released when we are together (the presence of Jesus) that can be felt as we worship together, pray with one another, learn as a group from the Scriptures, and share fellowship over coffee afterwards. There really is nothing like it, and there is no substitute for it.

So today we particularly send our greetings to Ackworth Community Church. Some of us have served together for 28 years, through thick and thin. Others have joined us on the way and become part and parcel of us. Some have only recently joined us but are already our close friends and valued members of the body. We miss you dear friends, each and every one!

No doubt you feel the same about the church you belong to. Why not tell them how much they mean to you?

27th April

LITURGY HAS ITS PLACE

When I was a studying at Bible College in the early 70s, I shared a room with another student called Eric. After graduation he went to manage a Scripture Union bookshop in the north of England. When we met a few years later he told me that he had almost lost his faith. What had saved him was his attendance at the local cathedral and his discovery of liturgical prayer. When he had no words of his own, he found that these ancient written prayers gave him words to say to God when he had none of his own to give. When he felt empty internally, he found a source of external inspiration.

Eric's words have stayed with me over the years and came back to me recently in my own struggles with prayer. I found myself yearning for a simple prayer book to sustain me through these somewhat barren days. Liturgy has two key benefits. It gives us words to use together, as a congregation, providing a common framework for prayer and intercession. But it also lends its support to the personal devotional life and therefore is not to be despised. It is not cheating to use the finely crafted words of others, words that have stood the test of time, as a means of drawing near to God and expressing our love for him. Sure, we don't want to be totally dependent on written prayers and fail to develop our own inner life, but there will be times when liturgy can come to our aid and carry us through those times when our own inspiration may be lacking.

I have been helped over the years by the Daily Office from the Northumbria Community, as well as Christopher Herbert's 'A Little Prayer Diary.' (4) I'm so grateful that our daughter Debbie managed to find my copy of the latter in my office yesterday. I know it will be a source of strength to me in my time at Cherry Trees. And perhaps you may also benefit from the help of a prayer book, whatever your spiritual background, in these testing times. We don't have to do everything under our own steam.

28th April

IT HELPS TO TALK

I wonder how you process what is happening in your life? Writing like this is one of the main ways by which I pull my thoughts together and try to make some sense of them, but I also find I need to talk as well.

Fortunately, I have several confidants who have been a great help to me in recent weeks - among them a psychologist, a bishop and a grief counsellor! That should be enough wisdom for anyone! Perhaps it shows the depth of my need. In addition, I have been greatly helped by your responses to my daily posts. This support I consider to be God's provision for us at this time. It benefits us both.

Having someone who will listen to us, and hold our confidence, is a great safety valve. I find that talking through my situation helps me to 'think aloud' and sort out the wheat from the chaff in my thinking. Listening to the response of my confidant can also shed new light on my situation, giving me insight I may not have by myself. It is also good to have my fears and concerns validated and acknowledged or perhaps gently challenged.

In these days of social isolation and times of great stress you may also benefit from talking through your thoughts and feelings with another person whom you respect. It doesn't need to be someone who is highly qualified, simply someone who you can talk to easily, who you know will listen well, and who can hold a confidence. A wise friend is a gift indeed. You may not be able to meet face to face, but you can use social media in many different forms to communicate with each other.

Being able to talk like this is vital for our mental health and spiritual well-being. Don't be afraid to ask for help or embarrassed to say, 'I need to talk.'

| 5 |

REFLECTIONS ON THE BOOK
OF RUTH

29th April

FINDING REFUGE

Shortly before we came to Cherry Trees, I had felt a nudge from God to read and study the book of Ruth. I brought a few books with me to help, but initially my emotions were all over the place and I could not focus my thoughts. I had to rest for a while and allow myself to be carried by God's love. Slowly my hunger for scripture returned and recently I have found great comfort in this ancient little story. It tells how God cared and provided for Ruth and Naomi in their need and desperation, and how even then his providential plan for them was working itself out in their adversity.

In particular the thought of God being our refuge, and our finding shelter beneath his wings, has sustained me and given me hope. At one point Boaz says to Ruth, "May you be richly rewarded by the Lord, the God of Israel, under whose wings you have come to take refuge (Ruth 2:12)." This Care Home has been for us a place of refuge and safety during these difficult days when we have been cut off from friends and family, from church and all that is familiar.

Furthermore, the kindness shown by Boaz towards Ruth has been replicated in the care we have received from the staff here, and which has moved us deeply. These hard-working and compassionate carers have often been devalued by society, but we have seen their true worth first-hand. But most important is the reminder that in times of need we can find a place of safety in God. He can become our source of security when all else has been removed. As Jesus said, he wants to enfold us in his love like a mother hen encircles and protects her chicks. We of course must be willing to turn to him for refuge. If we do, he will not turn us away.

By the way, do pray for God's protection on this place. I heard yesterday that this is the only Care Home in the Barnsley area without a case of corona virus. We want it to stay that way.

30th April

LIFE IN A FOREIGN LAND

During this time of being resident with Evelyn in the Care Home I have begun studying the book of Ruth, and it has spoken deeply to our situation. It is a story of love and loss, and of the providence of God bringing good out of tragedy. In other words, it is a book of hope for anyone for whom life is hard.

The setting is the time of the Judges, a bleak period in the history of Israel characterised by rebellion, disobedience and wicked sinfulness - not dissimilar to our own world. It seems that Elimelech and his wife Naomi, with their two sons, found living in pagan Moab a better alternative to staying in sinful Israel under the judgement of God through famine. The letter of Ruth breathes a very different atmosphere to Judges – here we find faith and love, loyalty and kindness, all generated by a living faith in God. It reminds us that at the bleakest of times God preserves a people for himself.

But life was not easy for the little family during their exile. First Elimelech died, then both sons, Mahlon and Chilion. How devastating this must have been for Naomi, and the two daughters-in-law. Their world collapsed and their future was in the balance. How would they respond? Would they turn to God in faith or turn away in anger?

We are living through a period of time when death stalks our land and thousands of families have felt its icy grip. Grief is the predominant emotion in 2020, and it comes in many forms, not just the grief of bereavement. Loss, and the attendant sadness, is everywhere.

For some there has been the loss of jobs and economic security. Overnight, businesses have failed, and careers been put on hold. Families struggle to make ends meet. Long-cherished plans for marriage, holidays and birthdays have been shelved. We have lost many of the joys of life like sporting events, nights out at the pub, shopping trips, meetings friends for coffee and so on. Social isolation has robbed us of our nearest and dearest and made us feel lonely and cut off. We have died many deaths.

So how will we respond? This is a searching time of both our character and our faith. We can become full of self-pity and turn away from God. Or we can recognise in all that is happening a wake-up call to our nation and the world and instead turn towards him again in humble repentance and faith.

1st May

WHERE YOU GO I WILL GO

When Naomi hears that God has once again blessed Israel with a good harvest she is keen to return home. Knowing she has nothing to offer her daughters-in-law, she urges them to stay in Moab. Orpah agrees to this plan, but Ruth refuses to leave Naomi. Her love and commitment are expressed in these beautiful words: "Where you go I will go, and where you stay I will stay. Your people will be my people and your God my God (1:16)."

We have heard many stories during the pandemic of this kind of sacrificial love, for example care workers moving in to live with their residents for weeks on end, or nurses leaving their families to stay nearer to their hospitals so they do not pass on any infection to their loved ones. There will be many other hidden acts of love that we may never hear anything about.

Evelyn and I have been married for 46 years, and we have shared so much together. We have travelled together, lived together and shared our faith journey together. When the time came for her to go into full time care the ban on visitors to such homes had just come into effect. I could not bear to think of saying goodbye to her at the ambulance doors and perhaps never seeing her again. My brother-in-law suggested I could also go with her as a resident, something I had not thought of, but which seemed to be a solution - if such a place could be found. A friend texted, "I hope wherever Ev goes you can go also." Then it worked out for us to stay together, first in the hospice and now at Cherry Trees. Where you go, I will go.

I hope I am not giving the impression that this was some great romantic gesture on my part, although I do love Evelyn deeply. It was the least painful option, but it has given us the chance to be together for longer, and although it is not easy, it is the right thing to do for now. I am also aware that for many the sacrificial part has come, not in being with their loved ones, but in being painfully separated from them in their hour of need.

I am sure you will have your own opportunity to express sacrificial love in some way during these unusual days - for your family, your friends and even complete strangers. It is interesting to see how in the midst of adversity love and kindness are flourishing.

"God is love. Whoever lives in love lives in God, and God lives in them (1John 4:16)."

2nd May

AN ANGRY GOD?

There are two common reactions to misfortune. One is to blame God (Why me?), the other is to blame oneself (God is punishing me). Naomi's response to her troubles is the second, to assume that God has caused her difficulties. "Don't call me Naomi (meaning pleasant)," she says, "call me Mara (meaning bitter) because the Almighty has made my life very bitter (1:20)."

Our theology is closely related to our basic concept of God. If we perceive that God is capricious, cruel, quick to take offence and so on, then of course we will assume any suffering we face is because he is displeased with us. This seems to have been Naomi's understanding. But is she correct? I think not.

She will soon come face to face with the sheer kindness and grace of God and begin to realise that God is more loving than she ever imagined. The Almighty is not schizophrenic, angry one moment and kind another! No, he is consistently good. Furthermore, to say that God was behind her misfortune is to say that the lives of Elimelech, Chilion and Mahlon did not matter at all – they died simply to teach Naomi a lesson. That leaves us with a rather grotesque view of God.

All we can say is that in a fallen world, bad things happen to good people as much as to anyone else. The death of the three men was not directly caused by God. Such faulty thinking served only to make her bitter, not better. She could have known the comfort of God had she believed more in a loving, merciful Father.

Our concept of God is always developing. For many this means daring to believe that God is good and kindly disposed towards us. This is especially important in times of suffering. Rather than being driven away from a God whom we imagine is upset with us, we can take refuge beneath the wings of a God whose loving heart waits to welcome us into the comfort of his grace and mercy. He is after all the Father of compassion and the God of all comfort (2Corinthians 1:3). We can comfort others with the comfort we ourselves have received.

3rd May

IN HEAVENLY LOVE ABIDING

A much-respected friend shared his conviction that God will bring something really special out of these present sufferings in my future ministry. I do not disagree but had to reply that at present I cannot see the future, it is shrouded in mist. It is as if there is no horizon to be seen. My work diary is testament to this fact. There are no entries for the months ahead, only blank pages.

I guess Naomi and Ruth must have felt this way as they trudged their way back to Bethlehem. They had no prospects whatsoever. Widowed and penniless, defenceless and vulnerable, they had no home to go to and no idea how they would survive. If only they had known what God had in store for them, they would have returned rejoicing with a lightness of step. As it was, they were downcast and weary, like the two on the Emmaus road. Naomi sums it up well: "I went away full, but the Lord has brought me back empty (1:21)."

This morning a hymn comes mind from the past that has rescued me before when all has seemed lost. I wonder if you have noticed during this period a revival of some of the classic hymns from the church's past, a searching for words and music with depth? 'In heavenly love abiding' by Latitia Waring (1823-1910) is worthy of such a renaissance. Convinced of the security we have in God's love during changing circumstances, she pens these heart-strengthening and hope-giving words:

Green pastures are before me,
Which yet I have not seen.
Bright skies will soon be o'er me
Where the dark skies have been.
My hope I cannot measure,
My path to life is free,
My Saviour has my treasure,
And he will walk with me.

I wonder if you feel like the future is shrouded in mist, that there is so much you cannot see? Let's encourage one another with the reminder that God knows the plans he has for us, not to harm us but to prosper us, and to give us a hope and a future (Jeremiah 29:11). One day, like Naomi and Ruth, we will look back in wonder at how he has woven together the strands of our lives for his glory. But for the time being, let's press on, one step at a time, trusting in the goodness of God and resting in his love.

6th May
FULL OR EMPTY?
Naomi's words have a deep resonance about them, don't they? "I went away full but the Lord has brought me back empty (1:21)." We feel her pain and her heartache. We sense her loss.

Of course she is referring not just to her financial status. When she and her husband Elimelech had left for Moab they were well-off, full of confidence, bursting with hopes and dreams. Then life had cruelly robbed her of everything and she was returning to Bethlehem humbled and chastened, emptied of pride and status, with her tail between her legs.

Naturally we would all prefer to be full rather than empty, but which state is more helpful spiritually? Jesus said, "Blessed are the poor in spirit for theirs is the kingdom of heaven." And again, "Blessed are those who mourn for they shall be comforted (Matthew 5:3-4)." The implication is clear. God's work can take place in us more effectively when we are stripped of the encumbrances of pride and self-reliance.

We are reminded that in the incarnation Jesus emptied himself, stepping down from the glory of heaven to take human form and embrace the disposition of a servant (Philippians 2:7). In so doing he demonstrated a vital spiritual principle, that the way up is in fact down.

Present circumstances have robbed us of much of the 'fullness', those things that normally make up our lives. We have all been restricted and limited, we all feel loss and grief. If we allow it, this emptying can create a larger space in our lives for God. And he can fill the vacuum that has been created in our souls.

In returning empty handed Naomi and Ruth placed themselves at the mercy of God. They became qualified for Divine Assistance, and soon they would experience the restoring generosity of the Almighty. They would discover his 'fullness', a fullness not based upon self-achievement and human accomplishment but upon divine grace and mercy.

Such fullness is available to us all, even if first we must be emptied. As the apostle Paul put it, "In Christ all the fullness of God dwells in bodily form, and you have been given fullness in him (Colossians 2:9)."

7th May

SWEET PROVIDENCE

Providence refers to the way in which God orders the events of our lives so that his good purpose for us is fulfilled in the details of our daily lives. Things don't just happen by chance or even coincidence. They are shaped by a Guiding Hand. This is a truth I have come to value greatly over the last few years.

The story of Ruth beautifully illustrates this truth. Indeed, commentator David Atkinson says that, 'If there is one theme more than any other which dominates the book of Ruth, it is that of the overruling providence of God, and our human dependence on him.' (5) And again, 'Providence says that God is there, God cares, God rules, and God provides. Faith in such a God undergirds every chapter of Ruth.' (6)

When the two women arrive back in Bethlehem their first concern is to find a way to survive. Ruth suggests that she might join the gleaners working in the harvest fields. The Jewish law made provision for the poorest people to pick up the grain left by the harvesters, so Ruth did what she needed to do - she went to join them in the back-breaking work. By chance ('it just so happened that,' 2:3) she found herself working in a field that belonged to Boaz, a distant relative of Elimelech, except she did not know of this man's existence or the connection between them. But it wasn't just a lucky break. She had been guided that morning by God and what began as a chance encounter would turn out to be, in the providence of God, a life-changing moment.

I feel our being here at Cherry Trees is providential. We did none of the normal planning or research that one would do before moving into a Care Home. We didn't visit the place, choose a room or read reports about its performance. We didn't even know where it was, and we were reluctant to come. There was no time, it was an emergency, and this place was suggested to us. Yet now we are here we can recognise that God led us and this is the right fit for us. We are even daring to believe that God has a purpose in our being here beyond receiving nursing care for Evelyn.

I wonder how you are discerning the hand of God in your circumstances at this time?

Probably some things have not worked out as you expected. Can you see how God has overruled? Perhaps some things have happened unexpectedly for the better. Can you see God's provision in that for you? Has God closed one door but opened another? What good is coming out of what has happened to you?

8th May

GENEROUS PROVISION

In the providence of God Ruth found herself in the right place at the right time. Even as she is gleaning Boaz arrives and immediately notices the young stranger at work in his fields. At this point all he knows is that she is a Moabitess with a reputation for hard work, kindness and faith. He is moved to help her in several ways, and the kindness of an unknown stranger is God's way of providing for, and protecting, Ruth and Naomi. It is more than they could ever have imagined possible.

Boaz helps Ruth in several ways. He provides food and refreshment for her and instructed his men to make sure her gleaning was unusually productive. He included her among his regular team of gleaners and made sure she was not molested. At the end of the day she returns home with a generous amount of grain, to the delight of her mother-in-law. Providence and provision seem to go hand in hand, and in these uncertain times we can take heart that God is watching over us too.

When Evelyn and I joined the Overseas Missionary Fellowship in 1975 it was a faith mission and we were required to empty our bank balance, small as it was, into the common pool. We learnt early on that God is our provider, and that he will supply all our needs. That does not mean it is always easy, or that we do not worry occasionally, but we do know that God can be trusted. We have learnt to live simply and to be content. We have lacked for nothing.

Way back in March we purchased a reclining chair because of Evelyn's decreasing mobility. Someone mentioned a local cancer charity might help us towards the purchase, so I sent them a short email outlining our circumstances, then promptly forgot about the request. Soon after our arrival at Cherry Trees we received a letter from them with, to my surprise, a cheque for £500. Not only was the gift a significant amount, but the timing of it reminded us that even here God will supply all we need, and not just financially.

Many of us will be conscious of financial needs at this time, with less income but the same bills to pay. Others will feel lonely and isolated, perhaps even afraid of what the future holds. Some will be struggling emotionally or mentally. Whatever our need God can meet that need, not in some magical way that requires no faith or removes any challenge from our lives, but in a way that means we must learn to trust him and wait for his good timing. A faithful God will not fail us.

9th May

TERMS OF ENDEARMENT

I'm learning a lot during this time at Cherry Trees. One important lesson for me has been how to address people warmly. This has come about by watching some of the carers here in their interactions with the residents, in particular two of the ladies on the night shift.

When Leanne comes on duty the first thing she does is to go down the corridor and knock on each door, sharing a warm word of greeting with each person. "Hi Margaret," she may say, "How are you tonight? I've missed you. It's good to see you." Her warmth and sincerity cannot be denied, and the joy in her voice is unmistakable.

Keeley is a bundle of joy and when she arrives the whole place gets a lift. She has a wonderful range of expressions that communicate love and acceptance - dear, darling, sweetheart, chicken, my lovely, to name a few. She makes everyone feel special, myself included.

I notice that Boaz also took time to greet his workers, and with a few well-chosen words communicate his appreciation of them and desire that they would be blessed by God. "The Lord be with you!" he called out. "The Lord bless you," they replied (2:4).

Psychologists speak about 'unconditional positive regard' as a basic attitude towards clients and I think as God's people we should do no less. How we address people matters. It should of course be natural and in line with our own personality, but if we can communicate warmth and acceptance, worth and value, then we will be speaking words of life.

That's not to say that the next time you see me you can call me 'my little chicken'. Context is everything.

PS You may not recognise me anyway. After so long in lockdown it feels that my hair is like Einstein, my eyebrows like Dennis Healey, and my tummy like Billy Bunter.

10th May

A GLIMMER OF HOPE

Ruth's report of her encounter with the kind stranger named Boaz stirs a memory deep within Naomi of a distant relative on Elimelech's side of the family with the same name. If it is the same person, then there is hope, for he would have the right under Jewish law to redeem them - that is to pay off their debts, buy back any land that has been lost and even take Ruth as his wife. "That man is our close relative," says Naomi, "he is one of our kinsman redeemers (2:20)."

A sense of hope is vital to our wellbeing in times of stress and difficulty. When we lose hope we easily fall into depression and despair. It is important that we can find reasons for hope to keep our spirits buoyant.

The very nature of God gives us hope, for he is called 'the God of hope' and the history of Israel was filled with examples of how time and again he came to the rescue of his people when all seemed lost. So the apostle Paul encourages us, "May the God of hope fill you with all joy and peace as you trust in him (Romans 15:13)."

Scripture also reminds us to keep hoping. The Psalmist writes, "Weeping may tarry for a night, but joy comes in the morning (42:5)." Yes, we will shed our tears, and the pain of grief or loss or sadness may linger but dawn will come eventually. We will find a way through, and light will shine again.

Even when it comes to death, the greatest enemy of all, we are not without hope. We can face bereavement and final separation with hope in our hearts because Christ has conquered death. "I am the resurrection and the life," he says, "He who believes in me will live, even though he dies; and whoever lives and believes in me will never die (John 11:25-26)."

Today is VE (Victory in Europe) Day, and in some form it will be celebrated here at Cherry Trees. This weekend the BBC are showing the film, *The Darkest Hour*, the story of Churchill and the Second World War. Despite its artistic licence, it tells a wonderful story of holding on to hope when all seems lost. At that dark time the songs of Vera Lynn gave hope to many soldiers. 'We'll meet again' is a classic expression of hope. And what is the ever-popular 'You'll Never Walk Alone' but a song to give us present hope in the midst of the pandemic?

The kindness of Boaz was the trigger that rekindled hope in Naomi and Ruth. We each have the ability to encourage one another through our words, actions and prayers. We can also encourage our own hearts too by choosing to trust in God in our times of darkness. The darkest hour is often just before the dawn.

11th May

A GOOD MAN

A few years back there was a lot of debate in church circles about masculinity and what it means to be a Christian man. We need look no further than Boaz to see faith at work in a man's life. He reminds me of Barnabas, the son of encouragement, who is described simply as "a good man, full of the Holy Spirit and faith (Acts 10:24)." In reflecting on his story in the book of Ruth, three things stand out to me about Boaz.

He is a successful man

He is described as a man of standing (2:1), a term which suggests he had done well in life and was respected in society. Boaz was not a priest or a prophet, nor a warrior or champion of Israel. He seems to have been a farmer/businessman who was hardworking and industrious and whose faith was lived out in the realm of business and commerce. This integration of faith and daily life is characteristic of a mature faith that glorifies God.

He is a spiritual man

His faith in God is real and deep and impacts how he treats his workers as well as the poor. He seeks to apply scripture to his daily life and to live by its principles with integrity despite the cost. His life is soaked in prayer and he brings the blessing of God with him wherever he goes. Any goodness or kindness he displays is a result of the Spirit at work within him. His character reflects the character of his God being formed in him, a God who is kind and merciful.

He is a sensitive man

Unlike many men, he is in tune with his own feelings and those of others. He is sensitive to the plight of Ruth as she gleans in the field and makes provision for her protection. When she comes to him at night, he refuses to take advantage of her vulnerability and seeks to protect her reputation. Sensitivity is not a sign of weakness, but of strength. Doing the right thing and protecting the weak often requires courage and great inner strength.

I cannot read the story of Boaz without being challenged as to my own spiritual maturity and the integration of my faith to my daily life. This is the same for each of us, whether male or female. The challenges of the present time provide us with a wonderful opportunity to live out our faith in a way that really matters and blesses others. We too are called to be generous and kind, compassionate and caring.

12th May
THROWING YOURSELF ON MERCY

I wonder if you have ever been really desperate? I mean so desperate and needy that you would throw yourself completely on the mercy of another person and shamelessly beg for help?

I'm not sure I have, although in coming to Cherry Trees we came very close to that kind of desperation. Certainly, we have become dependent on the kindness of others when it comes to Evelyn's care. We have nothing to offer in return except our gratitude. It is a humbling place to be.

Naomi and Ruth have come to a place of desperation, and the visit of Ruth to the wine press late at night reflects their panic. In the cultural context Ruth asking Boaz to cover her with his mantle was not an invitation to sexual activity but a plea that he would show mercy to her and act as redeemer (Hebrew *goel*). This audacious plan depends on Boaz being the man of integrity they believe him to be, and as generous as they consider him to be. They are not disappointed. Although there is a technical detail to be sorted out first (another possible redeemer with a prior claim), Boaz assures Ruth that he is willing to act as her kinsman-redeemer. "I will do for you all you ask," he says (3:11).

Mercy is one of the great theological words, but it is often overshadowed in contemporary Christianity by its sister word, grace. Yet mercy always comes first and precedes grace in the order of salvation. God is under no obligation to save us, and we have no claims upon him. We can only cast ourselves on his mercy and hope for his generous and kind response. That he is willing to take us under his wing is mercy; that from that position of acceptance he chooses to be favourable towards us is grace.

In coming to the aid of Naomi and Ruth, Boaz gives us an example of what it is to be merciful, a quality to be integrated into our own lives. If we have received mercy, then we must show mercy. The mercy of God, however, is far greater than anything shown by Boaz since it reaches to the deepest depths of human need, without limit and without constraint. He shows his mercy to 'thousands' (Exodus 33:6-7).

In the 1970s a new wave of worship began in New Zealand with the introduction of *Scripture in Song*. One of my favourites was based on Ruth 3:9 and expressed musically this casting of ourselves upon the mercy of God:

Cover me, cover me,

Extend the border of thy mantle over me

Because Thou art my nearest kinsman,

Cover me, cover me, cover me. (7)

Perhaps that is the response God is looking for from us today? We will not be turned away. He will cover us with his unconditional love and limitless mercy. He will redeem us. As we worship today, albeit in isolation from others, let gratitude for the mercy and grace of God well up within us again.

13th May

REDEMPTIVE LOVE

To take responsibility for another person's debts, mistakes and future is a big ask, but that is what was required under the law for anyone willing to act as kinsman-redeemer (Hebrew, *goel*). It was a costly undertaking even if they were able, but not all were willing because of the sacrifice involved.

In the story of Ruth we are introduced to a redeemer with a greater right than Boaz. At first he is attracted to the possibility of extending his land portfolio, but then draws back at the thought of taking responsibility for Naomi and Ruth, so he withdraws. He is able, but not willing. For him, they would not be a good investment.

This provides a sharp contrast with Boaz who is both able and willing. He steps forward with a guarantee that he will buy back any land that has been lost, pay off any debts, and assume responsibility for the future of his poverty-stricken relatives. Boaz, of course, is not motivated simply by obedience to the law (doing what is right), or by extending his possessions (personal gain). No, he is motivated to get involved by the highest motivation of all, that of love - love for God, but also love for Ruth, the young Moabitess. He steps forward to become their Redeemer, and bears witness to his good intention before the village elders.

In this great act of mercy and underserved kindness Boaz foreshadows the redemption provided for us by Jesus at the cross. Indeed, this Old Testament picture provides us with a rich insight to what God has done for us in Christ. He has taken responsibility for us by paying off the debt of our sin, by restoring to us all that has been lost by our foolishness and shame, and by making surety for our future. What grace is this! What a reversal of our fortunes. Those of us who had not received mercy have now received mercy!

The awareness that God in Christ has taken full responsibility for me has come home to me for the very first time today. Not only has he dealt with my past, but he has secured my future. He is my Redeemer, and he has not only paid off my debt but underwritten my present and future need. And all this because he loves me! Unworthy as I am, I am the object of his affection and the recipient of his generosity. He is the Son of God who loved me and gave himself for me (Galatians 2:20). And nothing can separate me from his love or his intention to do good in my life (Romans 8:28).

Wherever you find yourself today, in whatever circumstances you may be, take heart from this great truth and say with Job, "I know that my Redeemer lives (Job 19:25)!"

14th May
HAPPY EVER AFTER?

Every story needs a happy ending, and the book of Ruth closes with the marriage of Boaz and Ruth. How excited Naomi must have been to see what God had done for them and how far he had brought them. Her prayers had been answered.

Marriage is a covenant relationship made before God with promises and obligations. It is based on the covenant relationship between God and his people. Just as God loves his people with a faithful, enduring love (Hebrew *hesed*), so marriage is to be built around the security of loyal love. This is behind Paul's teaching on marriage in Ephesians 5:22-33. "Husbands love your wives as Christ loves the church," he says.

The New Testament has 3 words for love - *eros* (sexual love), *philia* (friendship love) and *agape* (sacrificial love). A good marriage has all three ingredients although at any time one may be more important than the others. As marriages mature with age, friendship and the willingness to sacrifice become more important.

After more than a month at Cherry Trees I have to remind myself why I am here. It is because of the promises we made to be with each other for better for worse, for richer for poorer, in sickness and in health. This is how our love for God and each other is to be expressed now. It is not at all how we imagined it would be, but this is the reality we are called to embrace.

Of course, being together in this way is a great privilege, and it has deepened our love. There have been moments of real intimacy when we have been able to talk in depth about things that matter. But most of the time it is quite ordinary, and we chit chat, sit in happy silence, watch mundane TV, talk to the carers and so on. Occasionally there are moments of mutual frustration! And so the days pass by.

I wonder nowadays if people enter into relationships too quickly and break them too easily. Our experience is that when we persevere at relationships, they become deeper and sweeter. But you have to persevere through the stormy, turbulent times to find those calm, peaceful waters! Every marriage will be tested.

I guess the lockdown period and working from home places a strain on the best of marriages as people are forced to spend more time together, and at close quarters. Hopefully that can lead to honest sharing and deeper communication that in the end will strengthen and enrich the relationship.

15th May

SEEING THE BIGGER PICTURE

I remember visiting Chatsworth House, one of Britain's most famous stately homes, and marvelling at the majestic trees strategically placed throughout the grounds. It occurred to me that whoever planted those trees had never seen them in their full glory. Landscape gardeners plant for the future, not the present. They know their work will be best enjoyed by generations still to come.

The story of Ruth and Boaz is wonderful in itself, but its true glory is in what happened afterwards. God blessed them with a son, Obed. He in turn had a son, Jesse, who became the father of David, the king of Israel who was also the ancestor of Jesus, the Messiah – great David's greater son. David Atkinson comments, 'it is in the ordinariness of the events of the lives of ordinary people that God is working his purpose out.' (8)

Our lives have meaning in the here and now and may well have significance that we are not aware of, some of which will only become apparent in the future. This is our legacy. We too live on in our children and our children's children. We may never know how our lives have impacted others, or how our example has encouraged them. Our words and actions continue to bear fruit. What we can be sure of is that our little story is part of God's Bigger Story. We have a place in history.

On a recent edition of Antiques Roadshow one of the presenters was shown a letter written by a soldier in WW2 to his young wife, to be given to her in the event of his death. Sadly, he was killed in action and the letter was delivered so that his wife knew of his great love for her. His descendants preserved the letter, and when she read it live on TV the presenter broke down in tears. Seventy-five years later she was impacted by the words of a man writing in a muddy trench in some foreign field who had no idea his words would live on in such a way.

Gaining this kind of perspective can energise us when times are hard and we fear nothing is happening. Our lives do matter, more than we realise. When we seek to live faithfully for God we make a contribution in our own small way to God's eternal purpose. Don't underestimate what God is doing in you and through you, even now in the ordinary events of your life.

| 6 |

CHERRY TREES (Part 2)

16th May

HOW LONG, O LORD?

If you are going to be awake during the night at Cherry Trees, 5am is about the best time. As day breaks, the home is unusually quiet, and there is a sense of peace. I lie awake and despite my concerns feel a sense of inner calmness. A good time to talk to God and to listen for the voice within. In the silence a question emerges. I find myself asking that age-old question, voiced by the psalmist and the prophet Habakkuk, countless other believers, and now me. 'How long, O Lord? How long?'

Sometimes time seems to stand still and the purpose of God to lie idle. Nothing seems to be happening any time soon and we become impatient for action, anything to break the deadlock. Yet we wait in vain, and the days pass without any resolution. How hard it is to live with ambiguity, with not knowing, with things up in the air. We long for resolution, for clarity.

I guess after 7 or 8 weeks in lockdown we are all anxious for things to start moving again. Our patience has worn thin, our self-control has reached its limit. It is a dangerous time. Unwise, preemptive action could be costly. But the pressure is building inside us.

Yesterday was the final posting on the story of Ruth. It has helped me deeply to work my way through this story and allow God to speak to me in my present situation through its words. But where to now? As I wrestle with the question 'How long?', the book of Habakkuk might be a good starting point, and I am reminded of a wonderful little book written by my friend Mags Duggan that is based on the prophet's words and her own wrestling with God in the midst of suffering. *'God among the ruins'* (BRF, 2018) might be a good starting point as our time at Cherry Trees continues, or for anyone who is perplexed by the question of suffering and God's seeming inactivity. Let's see what happens. How will today unfold?

17th May

WHEN TIME STANDS STILL

A youth club skit involved two bachelor boys. The younger was waiting for his girlfriend to come for their first date. What should he say to impress her? His older, more experienced friend suggested he say something like, 'Darling, when I look into your eyes, time stands still.' He thought this a great idea and practiced his line time and again. When she knocked at the door, he opened it but got all flustered. 'Darling,' he said, 'your face would stop a clock.' For which he received a well-deserved slap on the face!

It is strange how when we are enjoying something, time goes too quickly, but when we are enduring something, it drags. God, it seems, does not operate in a time-dominated way like we do and will not be subjected to any human timetable, hence our frustration. This frustration with God's apparent slowness or reluctance to act often boils over onto the surface in Scripture. Both Psalm 13 and the book of Habakkuk ask the question, 'How long O Lord?' Surprisingly, it is not considered impertinent to ask such a question of the Almighty, but a natural part of an open, robust relationship with a covenant God.

There is a difference between the two questions however. Habakkuk is frustrated by God's apparent indifference at the injustice that abounds in the world, a very valid query. The psalmist is more concerned about an apparent breakdown of trust in his relationship with God and is perplexed by the lack of merciful response to his cry for help. I want to start my mediations with Psalm 13.

A friend writes today and her letter has at the top 'Day 50 of lockdown'. I understand her feeling, and why prisoners often mark off the days on the wall of their cell. Time can move incredibly slowly at times like this. We have been at Cherry Trees now for 5 weeks and away from home for 6 in total. I seemed to be coping well, but today I am a little fragile.

For some there is an easing of restriction now, but for others of us our confinement continues and seems even more intense. And underneath it all we may well be asking about this, and other circumstances in our lives, 'How long must I live with this? Why on earth doesn't God intervene? Is he even there?'

It is a valid query.

16th May

GOD OF THE NITTY GRITTY

I want to interrupt the flow of my usual postings to share a really encouraging, if very personal and earthy, answer to prayer.

Wednesday and Thursday were difficult days for us. Evelyn has had a catheter for many weeks now since she is mostly bed-bound. On Wednesday it stopped working and had to be removed, with no replacement available. This was distressing for her. According to the nurse here, they had none in stock and would need to order another, which could take a day or two or even over the weekend.

Wednesday night without the catheter was a bit of a nightmare for Ev and the thought of this continuing was unpleasant.

On Thursday I checked with the nurse, but no sign of a replacement. I shared this situation with only one person, our friend Jackie (a prayer warrior) who encouraged me to contact the MacMillan nurse who had helped us in the beginning. That afternoon I phoned them, and the message was passed on, but someone called back to say catheters were only available on prescription, so they could not help. I was downcast.

The nurse here said she had now ordered a replacement but did not know when it would come. Jackie texted me, "Praying it will come soon." About 6pm the nurse knocked on our door and said, "It's come." "What do you mean?" I said, a bit surprised. "The district nurse had a spare one and she just dropped it off" was her reply.

We were delighted of course, at God's provision for us of something as down to earth as a catheter, but also at the sense of his loving kindness. Here I am asking "How long, O Lord?" and yet he still demonstrates his faithfulness to his unbelieving children. I can't say that I prayed in any way other than to lift my heart to God, but you have been praying for God to watch over us, and this is the result of that. Be encouraged.

17th May

VIRTUALLY CHURCH

Woke up this morning after a hot, restless night with the joyous thought that today is Sunday (I think, I hope, better check) and that later this morning we will be able to join our friends on-line for the new way of doing church.

I say join, but we won't see each other. This is no sophisticated Zoom meeting where you can chat to each other. No, we are limited to Facebook live, but at least we can see the names of those tuning in roll across the screen. It feels a bit like registration at school. Names are read out and acknowledged by our pastor and his wife. We are warmly welcomed. It is good to have one's presence formally recognised in this way. It never used to happen under the old way of church. Now we can work out who has signed in, and who has not (Why not?). The ones who are usually late for real church are still late for virtual church.

One or two people have to be guided again by phone how to join us since they have forgotten since last week. Welcome Dot. That's it, press the triangle in the middle of the circle. It takes a while; geometry is not her strong point. Strangely it feels like we have connected in this little ritual quite deeply, such is our starvation of human contact.

Then, when we have a quorum, the service gets underway. It's very much a low budget production. No montage of songs from the worship group, just Ash and Di live from their home (it's never been so tidy). Di plays the guitar, having come out of retirement and been retrained specially, and Ash will sing along if he has his glasses. We sing along too, although Evelyn lost the capacity to sing some weeks ago. Hopefully the mantelpiece clock has been hidden. It has a bad habit of striking 11 with 11 rather loud bongs during the sermon. But we are not aiming for sophistication. Last week most of the songs were too high for Di to sing or too low for Ash. And Cerys dropped the camera halfway through. But it's all good fun and feels like a normal Sunday at Ackworth Community Church (in case you want to join us, we are hoping during lockdown to increase our international audience by 100%).

We normally close the door to our room for this online event so we can hear properly, but last week the carers burst in right in the middle. It was like being raided by the secret police. They had come to get Evelyn dressed and lift her out of bed for the day. We have to allow this interruption because it is a bit like Heathrow airport here. If you miss your slot it could be hours before you get another one. For Evelyn, her mind a bit befuddled by her medication, this is a major disruption. She is so into the service she thinks she is really there and has gone to church in her nightie! Now the hall is being cleared just so she can get dressed. I gently explain this is not the case and she is reassured.

Ash shares simply but helpfully from Psalm 23, which has been a rich source of encouragement to us all, but especially for us. We need to be reminded of the Shepherd's tender care and rest in his love. Soon the service is over, and we feel sad. No time to greet people over coffee, but it has served its purpose and brought us together. With a click it is gone until next week.

I don't know how church will be post-corona. Some say it will be very different. I hope not, not in the essentials of warmth and love and joy and belonging and fun and laughter and knowing God. I can't wait for the first Sunday back. What a celebration that will be! Meanwhile I send our love to all our church buddies, as I'm sure you do to yours. Enjoy your Sunday.

| 7 |

REFLECTIONS ON PSALM 13

18th May

UNDERSTANDING GOD (Psalm 13:1)

By coincidence, as we return to Psalm 13, this week is designated as Mental Health Awareness week. After 8 weeks of lockdown I know I am struggling and asking, "How long?"

The first section of Psalm 13 (v1-2) is a list of 4 searching questions that come from a deeply troubled heart. They are questions not of an abstract theological nature, but questions about relationship that say, "I thought I could trust you." God's delayed response to some perceived need has caused confusion for David. He thought his troubles would have been over sooner, hence the heartfelt "How long O Lord?"

In his anxiety David perceives that God had forgotten him. "Will you forget me forever?" he asks (v1). What a terrible thing that is, to be forgotten by someone you love deeply, and whom you had thought loved you as well. The seeming lack of attention brings all that into question.

David also feels that God is ignoring him by turning his face away. "How long will you hide your face from me (v1)?" Imagine meeting a friend in the street, but instead of greeting you they cross over the road and walk on by. Is that person really my friend after all? Is God passing by, simply playing games with me?

These are David's perceptions, his understanding of the delay. But are they true? Times of testing often call us to re-examine our understanding of God. What is he really like? Can God be trusted?

Is it possible that God could forget us? It may feel that way, but the answer is he will never forget us. It is impossible that our concerns should slip from his mind. God himself says, "Can a mother forget the baby at her breast and have no compassion on the child she has borne? Though she may forget, I will not forget you (Isaiah 49:15)."

Is it possible that God could ignore us? Not at all. His face is always shining upon us in blessing, and the light of his countenance resting on us in favour (Numbers 6:24-26). Have you heard The Blessing UK song? Or the same song in different languages? Nothing that happens can change God's basic disposition to bless us.

We can in fact turn our questions into confessions, and this is my chosen strategy today:

- Lord, even though it feels as if you have forgotten me, I know you will never leave me nor forsake me.
- Lord, even though it seems as if you have turned your face away, I know that your attitude towards me will never change for I am the object of your love and favour.

These trying times may test our faith and our understanding of God, but they can in fact deepen our faith. An honest faith will be a more robust faith. A faith that has been tested will be a more enduring faith. And if we are steady spiritually, we will have better mental health.

19ᵗʰ May

UNDERSTANDING YOURSELF (Psalm 13:2)

'How long must I wrestle with my thoughts and every day know sorrow in my heart?'

The third question concerns the impact of God's delayed response on David himself, in particular his mental and emotional state.

In Mental Health Awareness Week we are being reminded that lockdown can take its toll on our well-being, and here we see evidence of that, although we may already know this from personal experience. The mind is a battlefield, and it easy to overthink the problems we face and become unduly anxious. In times of delay the imagination can run wild, usually in the negative direction.

Likewise, our emotions can run riot. David gives no clue as to the exact nature of his circumstances but clearly it had made him deeply sad, and that was a continuing state, day after day with no end in sight. Emotions should not be suppressed or denied, but neither should they dominate us in an unhelpful way. We can validate how we feel without becoming prisoner to negative emotions. These 'corona' days have brought grief to many, and grief has a myriad of different causes. We have all experienced loss and the longer this goes on the worse it seems to be.

How then can we manage ourselves in turbulent times? By understanding ourselves and our typical responses to stress, and by taking hold of both our thoughts and feelings. I do not pretend that this is easy to do for both are powerful forces. We can only turn things around with God's help, as we shall see later in the Psalm. We should not judge ourselves harshly if we struggle, for we are all human, and this is part of our humanity. But neither should we simply keel over and surrender to depression or despair.

Instead, with the help of the Spirit, we can surrender both our minds and our hearts to God. Here is my prayer today:

Lord you know my tendency to think negatively and imagine the worst.

Help me to take every thought captive and set my mind on your goodness and grace.

Lord, you know how turbulent my emotions are, and how destabilising they can be.

Help me to acknowledge them but find my joy and peace in you, not in my feelings. Amen

20th May

UNDERSTANDING THE ENEMY (Psalm 13:2)

The corona virus is often described as an invisible enemy. President Macron of France declared early on, "Nous sommes en guerre" (We are at war). Yes, we have a fight on our hands and it's more than physical - it is emotional, mental and spiritual.

David's fourth question regards his battle with his enemies: "How long will my enemy triumph over me (v2)?"

David fought many battles and had many enemies in his life, including the Philistines, King Saul, Goliath, even his own son Absalom. He seems to have been under pressure from some kind of physical enemy who – from what he says in v4 – actively sought his downfall. Whenever I read about these enemies in the Psalms it reminds me that we are all under threat from spiritual enemies – in particular, Satan and the powers of darkness.

Satan is no gentleman. He does not look at those of us caught in the pandemic with any compassion. He sees it only as an opportunity to add to our misery and bring about our downfall. He wants to see us frustrated with God and giving up our faith. I know that this is a time when some are turning to God, but I am also wondering how many will lose their faith when they are cut off from church and the usual means of support.

There are two ways by which Satan will come against us at this time of lockdown and isolation. Firstly, he will tempt us. He will push us into wrong responses to our internal needs. We may find ourselves seeking solace and relief in wrongs ways, for example comfort eating, drinking too much alcohol, gambling, even pornography or casual sex. Then he will taunt us. He whispers in our ear that God has forsaken us, that he is punishing us, that he no longer loves us. He will undermine our self-worth, saying that we are a failure, that we don't deserve God's love, that we may as well give up. He will rob us of our hope.

Fortunately, we know that Satan is a defeated foe and that Christ has won an everlasting victory over him. We share that triumph, and although we can't stop Satan from either tempting or taunting us, we can resist him. "Resist the devil," says James, "and he will flee from you (4:7)."

It is easy to overlook the spiritual dimension to our struggles, and to underestimate the opposition of the devil. Remember though that through Christ we have the victory. "Thanks be to God. He gives us the victory through our Lord Jesus Christ (1Cor 15:57)." We shall come through this. We will overcome.

21st May

TRANSITION - NEED A HELPING HAND? (Psalm 13:3-4)

It is easy to get locked into the darkness of our own thoughts and feelings. Sometimes it seems there is no way out, that we are trapped and held captive by our circumstances. We have no indication how long David stayed in the darkness, but it didn't last for ever as v3-4 indicate. Slowly his heart began to turn towards God again and once more he finds himself able to pray.

This happens not because of some supreme effort on his part, but because of an act of grace on God's part. There are times, thankfully quite rare, when we need a Helping Hand to come and rescue us, to save us from ourselves and lift us out of the mire. The change in David did not come about because he believed more or trusted more, but because in his helplessness he cried out for help. As the chorus says, 'Love lifted me, love lifted me. When no one but Christ could help, love lifted me.' (9)

I think today of Peter walking on the water towards Jesus, full of faith and courage, the model disciple. Then he took his eyes off Jesus, looked instead at the wind and the waves, and promptly began to sink. He could not save himself, but only cry out for help, "Lord, save me!" He needed a Helping Hand. What happened next? "Immediately Jesus reached out his hand and caught him (Matt 14:31)."

I certainly reached the place last week where I was crying out "How long, O Lord?" I wondered how much longer I could stay being here, but gradually there has been a shift taking place within me. Perhaps it's like a marathon runner who halfway through the race 'hits the wall' and feels he can't go on. Then, seemingly from nowhere, he gets a second wind and finds the stamina to continue to the end.

I like to think of it as the Helping Hand reaching out and taking hold of me despite my little faith. Grace at work in me, and grace available to each one of us to help us in our time of need.

22nd May
A WAY OF ESCAPE (Psalm 13:3-4)

God has promised that we will not be tempted beyond what we can endure, but that he will provide a way of escape (1Corinthians 10:13). The trouble is he knows we can endure more than we think we can. When we feel we have reached the end of our tether God knows we have not. But the faithful God is aware of our limits and he will not push us to breaking point.

David's cry for help, faint as it may be, is heard in heaven. He can still speak of 'The Lord my God' reflecting a deep personal relationship grounded in God's covenant with his people. Even when we are faithless, he remains faithful. David makes 2 simple requests.

"Look on me and answer me". He simply wants God to notice him, to be aware of him, to register his need. Hagar, abandoned in the desert with her son, was saved because God heard the boy crying. God opened her eyes to see a well of water. She knew God to be El Roi, "the God who sees me". Genesis 21:14-19, 16:13. Be aware today that our heavenly Father sees you, even as he sees the tiniest sparrow.

"Give light to my eyes". The second thing he asks is to have understanding of the ways of God, insight into his plans and purposes. This is not gained intellectually by working it out with our minds but is given spiritually by revelation. As with Hagar we need God to open the eyes of our hearts and give us the Spirit of wisdom and revelation (Ephesians 1:17-19). Then we will begin to understand why God is leading us the way he is, and what he is wanting to accomplish through our suffering.

There must have been a significant gap in time between v1-2 and v3-4, and then also between v3-4 and v5-6. Changes like this do not happen overnight. We have great need of patience, but such patience will be rewarded. I speak these words to myself, even as I write them to you.

23rd May

ANOTHER TWIST IN THE TAIL

After ten weeks of resistance, the defences against the corona virus here at Cherry Trees have been broken. On Monday, two residents tested positive. The same day Evelyn developed a chest infection for which she was given antibiotics. On Wednesday I also developed a slight cough. We were both tested on Thursday, and yesterday we had confirmation that Evelyn's test was positive. My result is still pending.

At the moment Evelyn will stay here and be barrier nursed, and I have to self-isolate in my room until I get my results. I will be allowed to visit her for an hour each day wearing full protective gear. This of course is not at all what we had imagined and will be hard for us both. Looking ahead, we don't know what will happen next.

Evelyn received the news with her usual calm faith. Her body has suffered so much over the last four years of cancer treatment. This will hit her hard. I can only pray for a peaceful and pain-free release for her.

Please pray for us over this weekend, but also for the staff. They are also being tested for the virus, and some will be under pressure from their families to quit now they have confirmed cases to deal with.

23rd May

THINKING POSITIVELY

Just got the results back from my swab test, and I too am positive for the virus. I'm not surprised since we have been in such close contact, and my cough was also very chesty. But I think I have a mild form and am taking Prince Charles as my inspiration (since he recovered from the virus) and the Lord as the ground of my confidence. I believe I have one more adventure in me yet to be fulfilled, so this is not my time. Which means I am up for the fight.

All day the trees outside my room have been battered by strong winds, not exactly a gale, but testing out their mettle. As I have watched them it occurred to me that if this were autumn the leaves would be blown off, but because it is Spring they are deeply connected to the tree and able to withstand the pommelling. I want to stay deeply rooted in Christ at this time and need the help of your prayers. I have been moved to tears by the messages of love you have sent us today. We are so blessed to have so many people bringing our needs before the throne of grace. Keep it up, please.

24th May

RECOVERY 1 : TRUST (Psalm 13:5-6)

It has been common during the pandemic to hear various governments give their road map for recovery, an outline of the steps they will take so that things can return to 'normal'. When we look at v5-6 we can see 3 steps on the path to David's recovery:

1. Slowly he begins to trust
2. Gradually he starts to rejoice
3. Eventually he can sing again

We do not know how long it took for the grace of God to heal David's heart. Certainly it did not happen overnight but eventually he starts his recovery. Slowly he begins to trust again. This change is indicated by the word 'but', a word of contrast - "But I trust in your unfailing love (v5)." He has made a choice to respond to the overtures of God's grace and leave his doubt and unbelief behind.

Trust is at the heart of any relationship and it is certainly central to our walk with God. We are called to trust him - to trust his word (that it is true), to trust his purpose (that it is always good), and to trust his character (that he is faithful). The circumstances of our lives will challenge and test the degree of our trust. Sometimes they will expose the fragility of our trust, but always, if we allow them, there is the possibility that our trials will eventually deepen our trust.

In his book 'Ruthless Trust', Brennan Manning suggests that it may mean more to God when we say, "I trust you" than when we say, "I love you". (10) It is easy to love God when all is well, but to trust God in the darkness requires a more mature faith. Trust has to be ruthless because it must resist all self-pity, the great enemy of faith.

I wrote these words on Thursday to be posted yesterday (Saturday), but events caused a change of plan. I didn't realise that by today both Evelyn and I would both have tested positive for the corona virus. It means I have to make the choice again, aided by the grace of God, to trust in the good purpose of God for our lives, and to rest in the wisdom of his perfect will. Working through this Psalm has prepared me for this. I feel no need to blame God or to complain against his ordering of my life. Instead I want to believe that his grace is sufficient for us in all that our situation requires of us.

This is a choice that you too must make in the reality of your life today. We can sink back into despair and doubt or we can take the first tentative steps on the road to recovery by trusting God, no matter how weak that trust may seem.

25th May

RECOVERY 2 : JOY (PSALM 13:5-6)

The road to recovery is a slow one, but once trust has been restored (however tentatively) gradually we may begin to rejoice again. No longer is life full of darkness, and no longer are we focussed on lament or even complaint. No, our perspective begins to change, and we feel the joy of the Lord returning. "My heart rejoices in your salvation (v5)."

This form of rejoicing may be quietly expressed initially. Perhaps gratitude comes first. Instead of seeing what we don't have, we notice what we do have; instead of being immersed in the negative we find we can appreciate what is positive. And we recognise that what we have is the result of grace, and not merit, hence our gratitude.

With gratitude comes thanksgiving. We must acknowledge the source of what is good in our life. All that is good comes from God and so we want to thank him. Past experience of his salvation, and the memory of previous deliverances, gives us hope for the present and future. Thus, a heart that was once weighed down with sorrow (v2) is liberated to praise again.

In talking about the importance of thanksgiving in the Christian life, Henri Nouwen reminds us that those who make a habit of thankfulness are not immune to the darkness, but they choose not to live there. 'They claim that the light that shines in the darkness can be trusted more than the darkness itself and that a little bit of light can dispel a lot of darkness.' (11) Again, we are reminded, that with God's help, we can recalibrate the focus of our hearts.

Today I have much for which I can give thanks. Yes, my life is limited in many ways, and not at all as I thought it would be, but I am still abounding in tangible expressions of the goodness of God. Both Evelyn and I are fighting the unpleasant symptoms of the corona virus, but we are surrounded by an army of believing friends praying for our deliverance. In the light of that I am choosing to allow the joy of the Lord to be my strength. How about you?

26th May

RECOVERY 3 : SONG (Psalm 13:5-6)

As trust is re-established and joy begins to return so eventually David finds he can sing again: "I will sing the Lord's praise for he has been good to me (v6)."

We know that the people of Israel when in exile in Babylon found that they had lost the will to sing. They cast their harps and lyres aside, a testament to their inner anguish. "How can we sing the songs of the Lord while in a foreign land (Psalm 137:4)?", they lamented. David too, here in the depth of his trial, found that his song had deserted him. The sweet Psalmist of Israel was silenced by his sorrow.

But darkness does not last forever, and now morning has broken in his soul again. O happy day! We should never take for granted our desire to praise God or the gift of worship that he gives us. Indeed, we need to cultivate both gratitude and thankfulness if we want to have a praising heart. The focus of David's song is indeed the remembered goodness of God. As an antidote to his depression he remembered the many ways by which God had blessed his life.

I am grateful to God that one of the ways by which people have ministered to me during this period of lockdown is by sending me clips of worship songs, many of which have helped them. Now music is a very personal choice, and not all have touched the spot with me, but many have, reducing me to tears of joy and thankfulness and hope. Music is such a gift from God, isn't it?

And the song the Lord gives us is to be enjoyed in harmony with others. From my early days in the Methodist chapel where I came to faith as a teenager, I have known the blessing of worshipping with others. It is one of the great absences in my life right now, a vacuum that is hard to fill. But one day we will be together again, and what songs we shall sing!

I look forward to singing God's praise with even more gusto and depth than before, for this is one of the by-products of times of trial. Our understanding of God's faithfulness, for instance, is greatly enriched by our experience of his unfailing love in the midst of our suffering. Out of the flames comes forth a love for God that has been purified like burnished gold. What a beautiful offering to bring to God!

This is the last posting in my series of reflections on Psalm 13. After this I am not sure what will happen but probably any future posting will be to keep people informed of our situation here as we and others seek to recover from the corona virus.

| 8 |

FIGHTING THE VIRUS

27th May
FROM THE BATTLEFIELD
Don't let anyone tell you there is a mild version of the virus. This is a beast and it is not easily defeated.

The symptoms I have experienced so far include a chesty cough, aching all over my body, and suddenly being gripped by cold shakes followed by hot fever. Far the worst symptoms have been a persistent nausea accompanied by a loss of motivation and an emotional fragility.

I am now experiencing lockdown within lockdown. I have to stay in my room 23 hours each day apart from one hour when I go to see Evelyn. This is not easy to do even for someone experienced in solitude. My room is very small and very hot with very little air circulating. I find it increasingly oppressive. I long for fresh air. I was doing quite well until Sunday when I became overwhelmed by the feeling that I could stay here no longer.

Monday was a bad day too and I began to look for a way of escape for the sake of my own health. I shed many tears that day as the enormity of my situation came home to me again. The last 8 weeks have taken their toll. On Tuesday I had a meeting with the home manager and shared my feelings honestly with her. She listened with great compassion and we managed to have the radiator turned off which has helped. She felt I would be better off here than at home by myself as I work through the symptoms of the virus. It is a good point and one my daughter Debbie has also made to me.

That afternoon I also went to see Evelyn who is now quite poorly. There is blood in her urine and we are waiting to discover the cause. I shared my concerns for my own health and she fully understands and is happy for me to leave should I so desire.

On Wednesday I woke with the usual nausea, lack of motivation and emotional fragility. After breakfast one of the carers came and said to me, "Come on, I'm going to take you outside for some fresh air." I put on my protective gear and went with her and then enjoyed 10 minutes in the morning sun. It was wonderful. I came inside and after a brief internet conversation with my son Alistair in Australia, lay down on the bed. I was soon overtaken by a very deep sleep the like of which I have not experienced before. I woke after three hours feeling refreshed and so much better. I'm sure it was from God and the result of your many prayers. I saw Evelyn again that afternoon and on my way back the carers took me outside again for the longest spell outside I have had for many weeks.

I was hoping this would mark the turnaround but in the evening I was overcome by cold shakes again followed by a high fever. I managed to sleep from eight until midnight but I've just woken up and feel the need to do something tangible, hence my writing in the early hours. So I am still not sure how this is going to work itself out. I only know I greatly need your prayers to bring me through so that I can stay here for as long as is necessary and do so with good grace, but that is a challenge.

28th May

I have decided I must leave Cherry Trees or I will not survive. I spoke to the Manager and she says it is up to me, but if I do leave I won't be able to come back. I talked things over with Evelyn and she understands my predicament. She seems to be less affected than me by the virus. We agreed that I should go home, a very tough decision for both us. We may not see each other again. We said our goodbyes then prayed together. I had no words, only tears, but Evelyn somehow found the strength to pray for both of us. I left quickly, the hardest thing I have ever done.

Editorial note

I gathered my things together, said goodbye to the staff, and went out to my car which had been parked outside throughout our time in Cherry Trees. Debbie came in her car to escort me home. Happily, the car started first time, and I drove down the driveway and onto the main road. Turning right I went straight into a traffic island which, in my poor condition, I had not seen. There was a loud bang followed by a long szzzz as the tyre burst. I pulled over to the side of the road to see the damage.

'Dad, do you want to go back?' asked Debbie.

'Definitely not,' I replied, then leaned over the nearby fence and was sick.

We called the RAC and a patrolman was quickly on the scene. He changed the tyre for us, and when the car wouldn't start, charged up the battery. We were so grateful for his assistance and set off again with me zig-zagging my way home. I took my things into the house and collapsed on the bed, utterly exhausted. I had no idea how ill I really was.

The next two days passed in a blur. I was still nauseous and fevered, but unbeknown to me my breathing was now being affected and I was gasping for breath when I spoke. Fortunately, Debbie noticed this. She had given me an oximeter to register my oxygen intake and also realised it was very low, so she called for an ambulance. They arrived within minutes, leaving me no time to take anything except the shorts and T-shirt I was wearing. For some reason I took with me my mobile phone and my iPad, but that was all. The ambulance sped off to the local hospital, its blue light flashing.

My memory is not too clear about what happened when after that, but I went from A&E to the Acute Medical Unit, and finally to Intensive Care (ICU) in a short space of time, moving rapidly up the ladder of care. I was just glad to have someone looking after me. I am so grateful to Debbie for her prompt and decisive action. She probably saved my life.

30th May

It's Tony's friend Debbie Hawker here. Tony has asked me to post that he has been admitted to hospital because of shortness of breath. He would value your ongoing prayers for himself, Ev, and their family. Thank you

31 May

Debbie Hawker: Tony has asked me to give you this update for your prayer please: 'Today is crucial. Must get oxygen back to normal. Trying an oxygen mask. If not put to sleep on ventilator'. Tony has also said, especially on this Pentecost day, 'Remind everybody that this frail body is the home of the Spirit. He is within me'.

A Poem for Tony

My tears fell for my brother
God's beloved:
Loved by me.
I poured out my heart in anguish

As if our Father could not see
His precious servant's suffering,
His precious servant's grief
So I pleaded with my Saviour
To bring him sweet relief.
But He'd seen my brother struggling,
And though He understood my tears,
He said:
"Barbara, let ME carry him"
And that
Is all I need to hear.
© Barbara J Parsons

1st June
Here's a surprise. I am allowed to sit up in bed for a while and feel well enough to say hi. Chest is the problem but will be given a new mask to wear, not pleasant, and also lying on my back.

2nd June
Debbie Hawker: Tony asked me to pass on this update and to ask for you to continue to pray. He is still critical, and he would appreciate prayers, he's in ICU. He's still on a mask not a ventilator as the ultrasound was encouraging. Staff are going to try and lay him on his chest for two hours today but he said it can make you feel like you can't breathe so is going to have to try really hard to last as long as possible. Please pray. Thank you.

3rd June
Debbie Hawker: Tony was well enough to have a little time without the mask during the night and to send a message himself. Good news! Please continue to pray for him and Evelyn.

4th June

Keep praying friends. Sitting up for a while. Pray for my lungs. Still on ICU. God can do this. Faint not. Tony

5th June

I need more oxygen in lungs. Make this a priority. Otherwise good progress. Can go either way. Tony

6th June

Yesterday's prayers made a huge difference. The doctor really pleased with my progress. Physio too, I was standing up unaided, now sitting by the bed. Will try without the mask tonight, it will feel like running a marathon. So valuing your love and prayers. Tony

7th June

Sunday morning. Christ is risen. I managed all night without the face mask. Still need the breath of God to breathe healing into my lungs. Do it Lord, glorify your name. Thanks for praying for me. I need inner strength and resolve.

8th June

Brilliant news, on the move from ICU to respiratory ward. On the mend! All praise to God and thanks to friends worldwide!

9th June

Wonderful to wake this morning with a sense of freedom at not being in ICU, but also of deep gratitude to God for what he has done in my life. I have no further news of Evelyn. Hoping the pieces of my recovery will start to fall into place today. I may have become diabetic through this experience. Still many challenges ahead.

10th June

Third day on this ward preparing to go home, perhaps tomorrow(?). Still trying to get my head around the diabetes issue and will talk with a specialist nurse today. May come off oxygen altogether. Evelyn continues to be at peace which is amazing in itself. She seems to have overcome the corona virus, which is unbelievable given her weakness.

11th June

Seeing if I can come off oxygen altogether today. So far so good. Staying relaxed about being here though, no rush to be home. Evelyn continues to astound those who speak to her with her lucidity and peace.

12th June

The doctor has just confirmed I can go home today!! How grateful I am to God and to all praying friends. A long road ahead of recuperation and recovery including 2 weeks of self-isolation.

STORM

Change swirls around me,
the sea dark with a rising storm;
but in You O Lord I put my hope.
Days melt and weeks dissolve,
tomorrow's horizon long obscured;
but in You O Lord I put my future.
Waves of trouble crash over me,
my heart founders, swamped by fear;
but in You O Lord I put my trust.
In quietness You call me to sit with You,
leave the shrieking storm in Your hands;

so in You O Lord I find refuge.
Around me, challenges still rage -
each stinging mile on a bitter sea;
but in You O Lord I renew my strength,
rise above the storm on eagles' wings.

©Christine Rigden

| 9 |

ANGELS UNAWARES

Editorial note
The story of exactly what happened during my time in ICU still remains vague in my mind. Many details have been forgotten, and the timeline as I remember it is probably not always accurate. During my recovery I became conscious of the people whom God sent to me during those stressful days to help and encourage me, messengers of his love and grace. I call them 'angels unawares' because they will probably never realise how significantly God used them to minister to me in my time of need. These postings, reflecting on my time in ICU, were made soon after I came out of hospital.

Angels appear in the Bible as God supernatural messengers and are mostly unseen by human eyes. But human beings can also sometimes act as God's angels. In Hebrews we read, "Never let your brotherly love fail, nor refuse to extend your hospitality to strangers—sometimes men have entertained angels unawares (13:1-2, Phillips)." In being kind to others we may actually be serving angels without realizing it. But also, I believe, people may act as God's angels to each other without knowing the significance of what they are doing.

During my time in hospital I was aware of four occasions when people acted as angels towards me, bringing me the message of God's love and reassuring presence without realising it. They were angels unawares. It was a scary and lonely time in intensive care. I was alone, without friends or family to comfort me. Yet God came to me through them. Their words and their actions were timely words of reassurance, tangible tokens that God was with me.

As I have thought about this today I have been very emotional. My tears have flowed as I have recalled what they did for me. It has taken me by surprise, but I guess it is part of the healing process still going on within me.

I have big gaps in my recollection of all that happened to me. Before I left ICU I was given a notebook in which some of the nurses wrote daily comments about my progress. It helps to fill in some of the blanks, and is very moving, but it is not complete. Perhaps I will never know everything; maybe I don't need to know.

I have been encouraged to journal my thoughts about this period of my life, and that is what I am doing. I process things best by writing, so if you don't mind, over the next few days I will share the stories of the four 'angels unawares', which I hope will encourage you. It seems to me that we all have the opportunity to act as messengers of God's love to those around us, whether they recognise it or not. And the best way to do that is by loving people and being kind.

ANGELS UNAWARES (1) - LOUISE

I was rushed into hospital on Saturday 30th May about teatime. I had already tested positive for Covid-19 and my symptoms were getting worse – cough, cold shakes followed by hot sweats, a terrible nausea that made me not want to eat, and a general lethargy. What I didn't realise was that my breathing was deteriorating, and I was low on oxygen. Fortunately, my daughter Debbie did and she phoned for an ambulance. In so doing she probably saved my life.

I was taken to A&E, then transferred to the Acute Medical Ward, then on to High Dependency Respiratory, before finally arriving in the Intensive Care Unit either Sunday or Monday. To use a footballing analogy, it felt like I was being rapidly promoted up the football league.

My recollections of this time are vague, but at some point, a young nurse came and sat with me. Her name was Louise and she had black hair, but the rest of her face was obscured by her protective mask. As we talked, for some reason I told her about my love of soccer and that I played Walking Football. She replied that she knew Bruce Dyer, a well know ex-professional player and strong Christian, well-known in Barnsley where I live. This suggested to me that she might be a Christian, so I asked her to contact Bruce and, knowing him to be a man of faith and prayer, request that he pray for me.

That encounter was a great encouragement to me in itself, but what was most amazing was that throughout our conversation *she held my hand.* In these times of no physical contact this touched me deeply and comforted me at a time when I was alone and a bit scared. 'Touch' is one of my love languages, and I felt God's love for me as I held her gloved hand. She didn't need to do that. No-one else did.

One of the verses I often use to comfort others is from Isaiah 42 where God says, "I the Lord have called you in righteousness; I will take hold of your hand (v6)." But how does God take hold of our hand? Sometimes in might be through an unusual sense of assurance that comes to us, but more often than not it is through the welcome grip of another person, a family member or friend. When Louise took my hand, it was in fact God taking hold of me at a time when I deeply needed reassurance that all would be well.

Having 'the virus' makes you feel like a leper. People are very wary of you, and even now I feel the suspicion that some people have towards me, even though I am not contagious. What was remarkable about Jesus was that he touched the lepers and healed them: "Filled with compassion, Jesus reached out his hand and touched the man (Mark 1:41)." Jesus reached out to me through Louise that night and started a healing work in me. She may not realise it, but she was God's angel (messenger) to me that lonely night.

I saw Louise once more when she dropped by Intensive Care when I was well on the way to recovery. She came to share my joy, and this time she gave me a big hug! I wondered if she ought to be doing that, but she was gowned up and no-one seemed to mind. I certainly didn't. I still don't know what she looks like. I hope to meet her one day to thank her personally, this angel with the black hair.

ANGELS UNAWARES (2) – ALAN

I found the Intensive Care Unit a very intimidating place. Happily, the peak in cases was over and there were only 3 of us in the ward designed for 7, so we got excellent one-to-one care. But the two people opposite me were both on ventilators, one for 20 days, the other for more than 30. As I looked at the bank of machines with their wires and tubes, and bleeps and alarms, I don't mind saying the thought of being put into a coma and connected to a ventilator terrified me. I cried to God, 'Please don't let me have to go on a ventilator'.

I also felt acutely alone and by myself, cut off from friends and family at a time I most needed them. Surrounded by people but knowing no-one. A stranger and an alien.

That first morning a doctor came to do his rounds. He was an older man and had a jovial, light-hearted manner which I warmed to straight away. Somehow his banter with staff and patients took some of the fear away and lightened what could have been a very sombre atmosphere. I listened as he gave the man in the corner a pep talk about getting ready to come off the ventilator and begin to get back to normal. The man was very cautious, but the doctor (who I think was called Alan) persisted in his friendly cajoling, and I found his words helped me as well.

Next, he came over to me. His friendliness put me at ease immediately. He told me he was an anaesthetist who had come out of retirement to help out during the crisis. For some reason he mentioned that he was a school governor in Thurgoland, a village between Sheffield and Barnsley. My ears pricked up. Thurgoland, you see, is where I go regularly for my Quiet Days with a small group of friends.

'Oh,' I said, 'I know Thurgoland. I go there for retreat to a place called Copster Barn. Do you know it?'

'Of course,' he replied, 'Chris and Helen who own it are good friends of mine. I'm on the Parochial Church Council at the church they attend in the village.'

I felt I had found a friend and an ally. He gave me my own pep talk then began to move on but before leaving me he said, 'I'll tell Chris & Helen I have seen you. And I'll tell our prayer group about you too.' It is easy nowadays to think that all mention of God is forbidden in the NHS, yet here was a senior medic telling me he would pray for me. How that lifted my spirits, and again reminded me that God had his eye on this little sparrow!

The next time I saw him I was starting my recovery. I told him the good news, that I felt I had turned the corner. 'Yes, I know he said, I have been keeping my eye on your progress every day, and we have been praying for you.'

By offering me friendship in this way, Alan helped me to feel at home. God sent him as a messenger to remind me that he has his people everywhere (there is no place where he is not), even at the heart of a frightening place like ICU. This particular angel was sent to help me believe I could get better, and to tell me not to be afraid.

That's a common theme with angels, isn't it? Chasing away fear and unbelief. It's what Gabriel did for Mary, isn't it? "Do not be afraid, Mary, you have found favour with God (Luke 1:30)."

ANGELS UNAWARES (3) – JEAN

I was much relieved that the doctors decided to treat me using CPAP – continuous positive airway pressure, a method of getting oxygen into the lungs for those who are able to breathe on their own but still need help. This involved wearing a large hood, like a spaceman's helmet, into which oxygen was passing. The one I had was bright yellow but had a clear plastic window so that I could still see my surroundings. I'm sure some people would feel claustrophobic being enclosed in this way, but I felt I could cope, and I determined to do what was necessary to keep me off the ventilator. If courage was needed, then I would be brave. This was my part in the healing process.

I'm not sure how many hours I spent wearing the hood. I seem to remember having it on at night and trying to sleep at the same time. It was very noisy as the oxygen was pumped in. I discovered that if I moved my head to one side I could make it squeak, and if I moved to the other side I could make rude noises (schoolboy humour I know!) It passed the time though. One day I spent 2 hours lying on my front (prone) which was far more difficult, and I was glad when that was over.

I found the nights were the hardest time, and I would watch for the first light of dawn (about 4.30) to know that I had made it through to another day. A variety of agency nurses covered night shifts and there was not much continuity. One such nurse was Jean, who as far as I recall came from Chesterfield and only did the one shift.

We must have had some conversation because she had written in the notebook I was given afterwards, 'I wish you a quick recovery. Nice to meet a person who has served the Lord in such a way as you. May He protect you and give you and your family peace at this difficult time.'

But Jean did more than that. At the side of my space helmet was a circular vent that could be opened to allow conversation or to give me a drink. As she came to the end of her shift Jean opened the vent and began to speak. She also held my hand and said a most beautiful prayer for me. Then she closed it up again and said goodbye. I didn't see Jean again; she was on just the once during my time on the ward.

I knew that hundreds of people were praying for me, and that there was a great wave of intercession each day starting in the Far East and finishing in the States. But this was the only prayer I actually heard, and it was special. God sent Jean that night to Barnsley Hospital so that she could pray for me in person, and so I could hear her prayer. She was a representative of all those others whose prayers I could not hear, although God could. She was an angel from Chesterfield.

ANGELS UNAWARES (4) – STEPHEN

Soon after I became more aware of my surroundings and began to recover a little, I asked if I could see the hospital chaplain. I made it clear to the staff that I didn't want the last rites! I felt as an expression of my own faith I should ask someone to pray for my healing, and the chaplain was the only person who I thought might be able to have access to the ICU. I knew the previous hospital chaplain, but he retired in 2019, and I was not even sure he had been replaced. I knew it would likely be a stranger, but that did not matter.

The staff tried every day for three days to contact the chaplaincy without success. Then, on the Friday, a young student nurse managed to get through and said someone would come at 11am the next day. Sure enough, on Saturday morning, right on time, a priest came into the ward. It could have been anyone, but it was Father Stephen from St Mary's church in Barnsley.

I had met Fr Stephen once before, when my sister Dorothy was dying, and I was with her. She belonged to his church, and she requested the last rites, so he came to the Care Home where she lived at the time. Now Fr Stephen is what we call 'high church' and I am very much 'low church'. We have very different approaches to church life and practice, but when he ministered to Dorothy I was impressed by the love and compassion he had for her, and his obvious sincerity. Afterwards we had a lovely conversation about our common faith. I felt then that although external things were very different, we in fact shared a similar love for God.

So, when I saw it was Fr Stephen I was overjoyed. It could have been anyone, but it was someone I knew and had a deep connection with. He remembered our previous meeting, and he showed the same love and compassion as he listened to my story and my request for prayer. He explained that he was not part of the chaplaincy, but occasionally helped them out, and that he was on relief duty. It seemed an amazing coincidence. So there, right in front of everyone, he prayed the most beautiful prayer for Evelyn and me. I felt I had been obedient to God and expressed my faith in him in a visible and tangible way as I sought him for my healing.

I shed a few tears I can tell you during our time together. That Fr Stephen should be on duty that day, and that he should be willing to come to the corona virus ward not knowing who he would meet, moved me deeply. But that's what angels are, servants of God, those who obey his will. And that day God chose to minister his love and grace to me through someone of a very different churchmanship to mine, a lesson in itself.

Niamh, perhaps the student nurse who had made the initial contact, wrote in my diary; 'The priest has been to visit you today. You seemed really happy about this and you stated it gave you hope!'

You bet it did!

ANGELS UNAWARES (5) – TIM

I wasn't going to include Tim originally, but I have decided to tell you about him. Tim came to the ICU as an agency nurse. I could see he looked nervous as it was his first time on the ward. When he was assigned to care for me, I decided to do my best to make him feel at home. We had a lot of time to talk, and Tim disclosed more about himself than anyone else had done. I think we both enjoyed our conversations.

Normally he works at another hospital in a big city as a Recovery Nurse, helping children after they have had operations. Intensive Care was really new to him and it took him a while to get up to speed and feel confident. He told me he had crashed his car and needed some extra cash, which is why he was doing agency work. He should have been on holiday in Spain with his family, but it had been cancelled, so he ended up in Barnsley instead.

What endeared me to Tim was that he was humble and chose to serve me in any way he could. Not only did he do the usual medical things – giving me my medication, taking my 'stats' and so on – but he looked after my personal needs.

By this time I was well enough to get out of bed. Tim helped me as I took my first faltering steps from the bed to the chair nearby. He sorted out my catheter when it got tangled up and understood that a man likes to stand up to pass water. He washed me from head to toe and wiped my bottom. He shaved me and made me look presentable again. He sorted out the hospital gown I was wearing to protect my modesty since I was in the chair for most of the day and on display. Nothing was a trouble to him. When I needed a drink, he brought me coffee. When I was peckish, he made me toast. He made sure that my lunch and tea were ordered from the kitchens, something that was often forgotten by others. He encouraged me when the physios came to see if I could walk unaided and rejoiced in my success when I did so. He continually told me that I would get better and soon be out of ICU.

Angels are sent by God to serve and minister to God's people, and when we serve other people we are acting like them. I am so grateful to Tim for the down to earth care he gave to me as I recovered. He helped me to feel human again, to feel so much better in myself. He got me ready for leaving ICU and the next stage of my recovery on Ward 17.

| 10 |

HOME

13th June

Wonderful to wake up this morning in my own bed, and in my own home! A good rest last night free from the noise of hospital. I was later getting home than expected (7.45pm), so it was great to be welcomed back by Evelyn's brother Ian, otherwise the house would have been in darkness. Have managed my insulin jabs this morning, so pleased with that, and already had a visit from the district nurse. Resting now on the bed and taking it easy. Hoping to speak to Evelyn this afternoon by phone.

14th June

I managed to speak with Evelyn on the phone yesterday with the help of the staff at Cherry Trees. She has done amazingly well in the last two weeks to overcome the corona virus and a serious urinary infection. She remains calm and at peace and content in her surroundings, and still able to have a lucid conversation. To be honest I never expected to be able to hear her voice again. Her recovery/stability is as miraculous as my own recovery, and again due to your prayers. We have both been blessed beyond measure.

15th June

The randomness of Facebook reminded me yesterday that exactly 3 years ago Evelyn and I had visited Holy Island and the ancient church of St Mary's where prayer has been made for centuries. It was a significant moment for us because we had gone there purposefully in order to offer our lives afresh to God for all that lay before us as Evelyn battled cancer once again. I remember it well but could not have told you it was 3 years ago to the day. For that I needed Facebook, but I think God was in the reminder that we had committed our way to God, and now we find ourselves at this point not as a result of chance, but because of the outworking of his purpose for our lives.

The timing of this random reminder strikes me deeply as yet one more expression of God's awareness of us. It makes me think, "How many of today's events have been influenced by yesterday's prayers?"

18th June

First time to sleep through the night. An essential part of the healing process and a good sign. For a while I have been waking up suddenly, fearful that my breathing might stop. I guess that is a legacy of my time in Intensive Care.

20th June

Just to keep in touch. I am enjoying this period of self-isolation as I recover from the virus, happily doing nothing much and resting plenty. I have been improving every day. Evelyn in the nursing home has been more confused of late as she battles yet another urinary infection. It is hard not to be able to visit her, but we have a daily phone call with her.

21st June

SHE IS MINE

Since coming home from hospital I have been acutely aware that Evelyn remains terminally ill in Cherry Trees, the nursing home. I feel powerless to help her since I cannot visit her because of the lockdown restrictions.

On Thursday evening I received a call from the home asking me to speak to Evelyn as she was disturbed and wanted to come home. I went over the reasons with her why we had decided together that the home was the best place for her, and that she needed 24/7 care that I could not provide for her here. She was understanding of what I said, and it seemed to calm her, but it was tough for me to say and underlined my sense of being unable to do much to help her in her plight.

Then, yesterday, I felt God speak a word into my soul, in the morning and then again, to remind me, in the afternoon. "SHE WAS MINE LONG BEFORE SHE WAS YOURS, AND I WILL NOT ABANDON HER NOW."

I realised that God had been at work in Evelyn's life long before I came on the scene. As her Creator, he made and formed her in her mother's womb, and knows her intimately. As her Saviour he has not only brought her the joy of salvation but come to live within her. As her Father, he cares for her more deeply than I ever could and has hold of her life even now. She is not alone because I am not there but is surrounded and kept by a Presence far greater than mine. And she is aware of God with her. She is not abandoned.

When we talk about placing someone into God's hands this is what it means. We hand the responsibility over to him. I am not able to be with her, but he is, and will be, every moment of every day, and every second of every night. She is held in his love, safe in his grip, still in that place of refuge.

I still struggle with my sense of helplessness and feelings of guilt, but this truth is changing my perspective and helping me to rest in the present circumstances. I feel deeply for Ev and having set out to be with her to the end, feel a sense of failure. But I now have a truth to hold onto that is more accurate than my feelings.

On this Father's Day, her heavenly Father is constantly watching over her. I can trust him with her care. He will not abandon or let down the child he loves.

24th June
MAKING PROGRESS
I have to say that I am delighting in these days of self-isolation! I love having no agenda, being able to follow my instincts, and having plenty of time to rest and simply to be. Each day I make a little progress, which is best seen when I look back to how I was when I came home from hospital just 12 days ago. Taking a shower then felt like running 100 metres against Usain Bolt, now it seems fairly normal. My voice too is regaining strength and losing the raspy-ness that was the result of my treatment. I am sleeping well, and no longer have the fear that my breathing may stop.

Whilst the first week was mostly rest and relaxation, this second week has been about accomplishing simple tasks. I felt the energy to switch on my computer and start to get my finances in order again after 3 months of neglect. I did my first cooking, some sausages in the oven, a major triumph for me. I have also done some washing and hung it out to dry (no ironing yet).

But I am in no rush to move forward, I realise it will take time. I will come out of isolation on Saturday but will not be rushing to the shops or anything. The next phase will be about increasing my stamina, and I hope to begin short walks and to recover some of the muscle that has wasted away over the last few months.

Evelyn continues to hold her own, but with periods of confusion and troubled by urinary infections. Monday (29th June) will be her 73rd birthday so we will send in a cake for her to share with the staff and others, as well as some flowers. It is good we can talk every day to her, and she continues to seem happy and at peace.

We do thank you for your continuing love and prayers for us.

26th June

Today is the final day of my self-isolation. I can hardly believe it's two weeks since I left hospital, but I have made good progress in that time, and I am ready now for phase 2 of my recovery - regaining stamina and building up muscle. I am looking forward to taking short walks again, but only slowly to begin with. Also, to joining Debbie and family in our 'bubble', and slowly getting accustomed to life 'out there' which I haven't experienced for three months.

I took the car out for a short drive and only hit the curb once! That's a big improvement on my last journey when I left Cherry Trees but shows I have still a lot of things to get used to again.

On Monday Evelyn will be 73 and Debbie and I will be able to visit her for the first time. The staff of Cherry Trees will bring her out to the balcony area so we can chat with her from a distance. We are hoping the weather will be fine in the Barnsley area around 10.30am. A lot to look forward to!

26th June

SHOCKED to hear that 7 members of staff at Cherry Trees have been arrested for neglect of residents. This precedes our time there, and Evelyn is in no way affected. I am almost certain that it does not relate to the nursing unit that Evelyn is on. As you know, we have had nothing but praise for the Care Home staff, and in my time there I saw nothing to raise an alarm. It is a big place, on 3 levels, so we only saw a fraction of the place. We remain happy with Evelyn's care, and we don't anticipate her moving, but this is a huge blow to the home, and the majority of the kind-hearted, hardworking staff employed there. It has been on BBC local news, so I thought you would want to know our perspective. (Editorial note: Subsequently all charges were dropped.)

28th June

Today is Sunday, when we remember the resurrection of Christ, and the start of a whole new way of living.

During the 3 months the house has been empty many of the potted plants in our little garden did not survive the lack of watering during one of the hottest Springs on record, but one did - a hardy, old rhododendron which is now showing its full glory right outside my office. It is a symbol to me of recovery and restoration and of the power of the new life within us to make a comeback. If the going is tough today, don't despair. Better days are ahead. As Gloria Gaynor sings, the message is, "I will survive".

29th June

Just back from a very satisfying visit with our daughter Debbie to see Evelyn on her birthday. Despite it being grey and overcast, and not very warm, the staff were able to bring Evelyn out onto the balcony for a short time. I must admit I was both excited and nervous, but it was easier than expected, and a happy time. We handed over lots of flowers and gifts from ourselves and others, and although a little bewildering for her, Evelyn enjoyed seeing us in person for a short time. We also delivered gifts for the staff, which were greatly appreciated after the difficulties the home has been through. Alistair joined us briefly by FaceTime from Australia. It looks as if we may be able to visit again in the near future, which would make such a difference.

1st July

A breath of fresh air

As part of my recovery I have now started taking a short walk each day to build up my stamina and restore my fitness. I have enjoyed being out in the open air, the first time in over 3 months. In particular on these blustery days I have been surprised to find how much I am enjoying the wind, and the joy of being able to feel it enter my lungs.

It reminded me about my time in Intensive Care when I was fighting for breath and having oxygen pumped into my lungs. I remember that it was Pentecost Sunday, the day when the Holy Spirit, the wind (or breath of God) came sweeping into the church, filling it with new life. As I lay in bed, I asked that God would fill my lungs with his divine life, that he would breathe into me his own breath and heal me. It was one of the few times I was able to pray clearly and distinctly.

We are all dependent on God for the breath we breathe. We should never take it for granted. Afterwards, when I was recovering, I came across this song by *All Sons and Daughters* that has the chorus:

It's Your breath in our lungs

So we pour out our praise

We pour out our praise

It's Your breath in our lungs

So we pour out our praise to You only

At creation we read how God made the first man from the dust and then breathed into his nostrils the breath of life (Genesis 2:7). What a special gift that is, and how wonderful to be daily filled with the Spirit (breath) of God so that we can praise him with our whole being.

Today, don't take your breathing for granted. Savour every breath and thank God for his Spirit within you.

5th July

I went on my own to see Evelyn today, meeting outside on a cold and cheerless day. It was a sobering experience as she seems to have declined a great deal, slumped in her wheelchair and unable to make any real response or conversation. I didn't stay long as it was obviously not doing her much good. I came home very sad indeed.

10th July

CARRIED TO JESUS

People have asked me what lesson have I learned through my experience with the corona virus? I guess the one thing that stands out to me it that in my helplessness I found myself carried by God, and by the prayers of his people.

It was touch and go and my treatment involved spending hours receiving oxygen from a CPAP mask, on my back, and in the prone position. All this while I discovered I had little energy to pray and no voice with which to sing, not that I could remember many words of even the most familiar hymns. I had imagined that if I were ever in a situation of great need I would be able to pray and praise my way through. In reality I could do little help myself. It was a lonely and frightening place to be.

The story of the paralysed man (Mark 2:1-5) came into my mind. He too could do nothing. He had to be stretchered to Jesus by his friends, who had to be determined enough to break through the roof so that he might be healed. I felt all I could do was to allow myself to be carried on the prayers of others.

I was aware that many people, all over the world, were praying for me. It was as if a global tide of prayer was offered on my behalf, starting in SE Asia, continuing through the Middle East and Europe, and on into America. While some were praying, others slept, but I was continually being brought before the throne of grace, stretchered into the presence of God by an army of friends who were determined I would pull through.

Some could only pray with tears, literally crying out to God for me. Others were woken in the night with specific prayers on their hearts. Small groups prayed together using Zoom; people I know, and people I didn't.

Eventually I turned the corner and began to get better. After nine day in the ICU I was transferred to a recovery ward. What a joyful day that was! Then five days later I was allowed home. I have since spent two weeks in self-isolation and am getting stronger every day. It will be a slow process, and I am trying not to rush things.

As I reflect on my experience, I realise there is a depth of suffering that brings us to a place of utter weakness where we are cast upon God and the prayers of his people. We cannot battle through by ourselves; we need the help of others. How grateful I am for friends like you who stretchered me to Jesus and by their determination broke through the roof of sickness to place me at the feet of Jesus where healing could be found.

Since being at home I watched a documentary about the singer-songwriter Carole King. Perhaps her most famous song is 'You've Got A Friend'. Do you know it? Listen to it if you can, it is a great reminder of the value of friendship which we should never take for granted.

11th July

Sad to say that Evelyn is now in the final stages of her earthly life. We were called to her bedside last night. Our daughter Debbie, her brother Ian, and I were able to spend the whole day with her today. She is sleeping peacefully but aware of us when she wakes. It is so good to be at her side again, and in Room 16 where we spent so much time together. The circle is complete. Our pastor, Ashley Guest, came to pray with her that she might now be released from her suffering into God's eternal rest. Pray that she will be at peace as she makes her way to Glory. "For me to live is Christ, to die is gain (Philippians 1:21)."

13th July

Evelyn went to be with the Lord peacefully this morning about 2am. Last night as I said goodbye to her and prayed with her, I reminded her that she would soon be in heaven, that the angels would escort her, and that Jesus would be waiting to greet her. Throughout the prayer she said 'Amen', then suddenly prayed herself: 'Thank you Jesus you have led me all the way.' Those were her last words. She slipped peacefully away in her sleep a few hours later, taking even the care staff by surprise. As a family we are so grateful for your prayers and love.

26th July

Yesterday's Thanksgiving for Evelyn brought us great comfort. We are grateful for the technology that make it possible for us to connect with friends worldwide, from Australia and the Far East, and from Bermuda and the United States. Listening to people share their memories of her did us a lot of good. Thanks to those who took part, and to all who chose to be involved. It seems amazing that only a few months ago we had not heard of Zoom, and the idea of linking up in this way would never have been in our minds.

Next will be the funeral on Tuesday, and I am not expecting it to be easy. At the moment I think I am still in the unreality stage in my grieving. It seems as if we have reverted to that period when I was at home and Evelyn was still in the nursing home - still there but not contactable. The funeral will be a stark reminder that she has gone. But I am encouraged that so many friends want to come to the graveside even in these difficult times for social interaction. It will be another significant moment in our journey and your prayers are appreciated.

By the way, thank you for so many beautiful cards and messages at this time. I have read each one and been strengthened by knowing you care.

29th July

The funeral yesterday was all we hoped it would be, and together with the Zoom Thanksgiving on Saturday made us feel we had given Evelyn a good send-off and celebrated her life really well. It was a real encouragement to see about 70 people (socially distanced) at the graveside on a sunny but blustery day when the rain stayed away. Ashley Guest, our pastor and long-time friend, did a great job of leading the service, and he summed up Evelyn's life really well. The most moving part was when people brought flowers from their own gardens and placed them on the coffin, such a lovely tribute to a lady who loved her garden so much. Given all the restrictions and limitations around social gatherings and funerals at present I think we did better than expected. Thanks to all who came, and those who were thinking and praying for us yesterday.

5th August

Good news from the doctor today - recent X-ray shows lungs all clear. Medical skill + worldwide prayer = miracle. Thanks to God and all involved.

| 11 |

EPILOGUE

As I look back on the journey of the last few months it is not with a sense of trauma, but a feeling of privilege. Of course, it was traumatic, but the mind has an amazing way of healing itself and moving on. There were days when it was really tough, and I would not want to walk that path again. Yet throughout the ordeal I mostly enjoyed a real sense of God's presence and saw him at work in our situation in extraordinary ways. That is why in retrospect I am left with a sense of privilege. His plans for us both were being worked out, and they were plans for good as he said they would be (Jeremiah 29:11).

The words of the apostle Paul that describe his personal dilemma about his own future, and which became our watchword over the past months, stand true today: "For to me, to live is Christ and to die is gain (Philippians 1:21)." He describes the tension he felt when imprisoned and facing a possible death sentence – the tension between dying and being with his Lord and staying alive and continuing his ministry. Since his conversion on the Damascus road his whole life had been lived for one single purpose, that Christ might be exalted (magnified) in everything he did (v20). With that perspective on life, death could be seen as a welcome departure for a better place, a gain not a loss. As it happened, he did not die at that time but continued his fruitful ministry on earth.

For Evelyn, whose whole life from childhood had been lived with a similar aim of glorifying God and doing his will, death came as a welcome release from much suffering. Her departure from this life of serving Christ has to be balanced with the joy she now has in seeing Christ and being with him. In this sense, while we feel the loss, she is experiencing the gain – no more suffering or pain, only the glory of heaven itself.

For me, who shares that same desire that Christ might be glorified in my life, there is the possibility of further adventure with God. I came close to death, but I have been spared so that I may continue to fulfil the purpose God has for me. Exactly what that looks like will become clearer in the days ahead. What I do know is that the Saviour who led Evelyn all the way, will continue to lead me until my life's work is done. The challenge now is to come to terms with her passing and, with God's help, to rebuild my life.

References

1. Bible Reflections for Older People, May-August 2020, Bible Reading Fellowship p12

2. David Atkinson, The Message of Ruth, Inter-Varsity Press 1983, p14

3. Bible Reflections for Older People, p16

4. Christopher Herbert, A Little Prayer Diary, Harper Collins 1966

5. David Atkinson, p122

6. David Atkinson, p14

7. David & Dale Garratt, Prepare ye the Way Part 2

8. David Atkinson, p126

9. Written by American gospel singer, Alan Jackson

10. Brennan Manning, Ruthless Trust, SPCK 2002, p181

11. Henri Nouwen, Return of the Prodigal, DLT 1994, p117

Lightning Source UK Ltd.
Milton Keynes UK
UKHW022023251020
372231UK00003B/50